MW00699835

CHANGE DOESN'T
BITE

Drew M. Sandler

A STORY OF A DOG, A TEAM BY THE
BAY, AND HOW TO CHANGE YOUR WAY

CHANGE DOESN'T
BITE

www.changedoesntbite.com

Drew Y. Sanders
FORWARD BY JOE EHRMANN

Change Doesn't Bite: A Story of a Dog, a Team by the Bay, and
How to Change Your Way
Copyright © 2012 by Drew Yager Sanders

www.changedoesntbite.com

All rights reserved. No part of this book may be used or repro-
duced, stored or transmitted in any manner whatsoever without
written permission from the writer or publisher, except in the case
of brief quotations embodied in critical articles and reviews.

TABLE OF CONTENTS

FOREWORD

BY JOE EHRMANN

In 2003 my friend Jeffrey Marx told me about a group of people in California that had formed a nonprofit that would send a copy of the book "Season of Life" to any coach or parent that wanted to use the teachings of the book but couldn't afford a copy. The book was about a team that I was coaching and Jeffrey was the author. The book ended up being quite successful, and we were speaking on a regular basis to coaches everywhere. Often times we would meet a coach from an impoverished area who need ten copies for his coaches and at times like that we were fortunate enough to know that we could always say yes to that coach.

At the center of that movement was Drew Sanders and every time we needed books, Drew found a way to raise the needed funds and get free copies of the books to people in need. 7 years later and with a strong friendship now built, when my own book "InSideOut Coaching" was published I reached out to Drew and again his California Season of Life Foundation was there with support for our countries coaches in need.

When Drew told me he was writing a story I encouraged him to go for it and I was only too pleased to end up being one of the characters. The main character in Drew's story, Sam, represents so many of us in our struggles with the changes in our lives. All of us could use more mentors, and I for one try to never miss a chance to mentor or encourage a friend in need. Drew has become a friend, mentor and inspiration to me and I am excited that now you too will have the opportunity to experience Drew's perspective and wisdom.

I hope you enjoy this quick walk through the 2010 San Francisco Giants Season as seen through the eyes of Sam and the mentors he meets on the way to AT&T Park.

INTRODUCTION

Welcome to this short story about a six year old chocolate lab named Sam who lives in San Francisco and is a diehard Giants fan. Sam thinks his life is all set up just the way he wants it, and then he loses his best friend, Larry.

Much of Sam's certainty comes from Larry's vision of how to live life well. The only problem is that Larry is a pug, and, while pugs and Labrador retrievers are both dogs, much of the similarities end there. Of course, Sam has no concept of this, as Larry has been his only mentor. Once Larry leaves, Sam is unsure of what to do. Fortunately, he is saved by the beginning of the 2010 baseball season, and, in honor of Larry, he heads to AT&T Park.

Sam's trips to "The Yard" become a series of adventures and chance encounters with a distinct group of mentors. Each of the mentors alters Sam's perspective on life. They share their insights and life lessons, using the Giants players and their games as examples.

The city of San Francisco, and some of its lesser known treasures, is the back drop for this story about learning how to deal with the changes that we all face.

Be you a lover of baseball, the San Francisco Giants, or the city by the Bay, this story will walk you through what, for many, was a fantastic seven month Giants season.

Hopefully, one or two of the mentors will speak to you in some way, and, regardless of your current position in life, you will jump into the character of Sam. His journey, like yours, is never point A to point B. In fact, sometimes Sam's life looks like that famous San Francisco landmark known for its sharp turns. Yes, life can often feel like Lombard Street!

Enjoy the ride!
Drew Y. Sanders

CHAPTER 1

Sam

"You gotta be a man to play baseball for a living,
but you gotta have a lot of little boy in you too."
–Roy Campanella

San Francisco in February is a city in the midst of several seasonal changes. The rain can come down for days on end, the Chinese New Year parades litter the city streets with lights and confetti, and the die-hard baseball fans count down the days to when pitchers and catchers report to spring training. Baseball in San Francisco got a real boost in 1958, when Horace C. Stoneham moved the New York Giants from the Polo Grounds of upper Manhattan to Seal Stadium at the corner of Bryant and Sixteenth. Willie Mays, "The Say Hey Kid," was the star attraction as the starting center fielder, and the San Francisco Giants Baseball Club was formed.

Fifty-two years later, and with no World Series titles to claim, the fan base was loyal, charismatic, and weathered. On the positive side, the new ballpark, "The House that

Barry Built," was a dramatic improvement over Candlestick Park, and the team was only seven outs away in game six from winning the 2002 World Series. These, along with some great individual events and Hall of Fame players, were the highlights. Yet the city by the bay, the city of change, the city of acceptance, and the ultimate city of creativity couldn't seem to get their hands on the Commissioners Trophy. Chief among these fans, and at the front of the line every year for his season ticket, was Sam, a six year old chocolate Labrador retriever who lived with his family in a "Rousseou Flat" in the Marina.

Sam had lived in San Francisco ever since his family had bought him from a breeder as a puppy. He came from a long line of excellent water dogs. Hunting and working in and around the water were his best natural traits. However, growing up in a flat in the city with a few young children had made Sam a bit more domesticated, and the closest he got to the water were his walks to Fort Mason and the occasional run along the beach at Crissy Field. Still, Sam had no complaints. He had his family, his routines, his San Francisco Giants, and, most of all, his mentor and best friend, Larry.

Larry was a ten year old pug, who, unlike Sam, was made for city life. His stature and short legs made running for long periods of time very difficult. Strutting around the house or down the crowded Chestnut Street and looking regal were exactly his cup of tea. Sam and Larry had met five years ago when Sam's family moved into the lower flat at 1117 Bay Street. Larry, typically very reserved with strangers, knew that there was no avoiding knowing Sam, as he was in the building and they shared a common backyard. For Larry, the big city of San Francisco was very small, and that was how he liked it. He would have to train Sam a bit to make this predictably rambunctious breed tolerable as his flat mate.

As an impressionable and large footed one year old, Sam was bumping into everything in and out of the house, and he couldn't quite figure out how not to get into trouble on his walks with his owner and the baby stroller. For some reason, he always smelled something amazing just up ahead and would forget he was on a leash. Then he would become fixated on a new smell on the other side of the side walk. Sadly, this would occur just as his owners had one hand on the stroller, one on his leash, and all while juggling a cup of coffee from Peets. One false move by Sam and the cup of coffee was inevitably spilled, causing the baby to cry.

Worse yet, for some reason, was Sam's tremendous curiosity when it came to other humans and animals. His unabashed openness led him directly to whatever or whomever he met with a smile, a wag of the tail, and maybe even a paw or two for good measure. The paws on humans didn't exactly work too well from the humans' perspective, and neither did his poorly located nose sniffs. It appeared that Sam had a problem.

Larry, the older and wiser pug, was quick to point out to Sam that, if he didn't want to always be getting in trouble, he had better learn the ways of city life.

Larry really believed and lived by these mottos, and his life was just fine. Sam, being far away from his natural environment and appearing like he was always one step away from the pound, decided to follow Larry's lead.

"Larry's Laws" for city life helped out Sam quite a bit, and his owners were very excited to see that some of "the puppy" had gone out of him. Sam was given a few more privileges and, in fact, was allowed to have his own doggy door to the back yard. He was even given his very own dog house right next to Larry's. Hanging out in the backyard with Larry was where Sam learned about the great game of baseball and that San Francisco had a home team named the Giants.

Larry's doghouse was different than Sam's. It was more of a palace really, and it had its own radio. Sam's was very plain in comparison; it was a Petco special that didn't really smell like anything. The good news was that at least Sam could hear the game coming from Larry's house.

Larry appeared to know everything about baseball, and his radio was tuned to the Giants' flagship station, KNBR 680, all the time. Murph and Mac, Gary and Larry, Fitz and Brooks, The Razor and Mr. T – he knew them all. In fact, he had a picture of himself and the Giants' play by play announcers, Kruk and Kuip, right next to the radio from the last time the Giants had the dog day game.

DOG PATCH

Sam learned the laws of baseball from Larry in their backyard. The game had an endless series of situations, and there was always one right thing to do. Larry seemed to know them all, and listening to the away games with him was an exercise in listening to two conversations at once. Sam had to be able to listen to the game and then listen to Larry explain what "The Book" said to do in that situation. If another team made a mistake and the Giants benefited, Larry would smile at Sam and say, "It's all about the fundamentals Sam."

However, if a Giants' player or manager went against "The Book," Larry would howl and call for that person's head, and the next day he would listen anxiously to the radio to make sure all the other callers agreed with him.

The home games were a different story. When Sam was three years old, he had shown enough ability to obey and follow the rules of Larry that his owners presented him with a season pass to the Dog Patch at AT&T Park. He was now allowed to go to the games with Larry. This was a huge step for Sam. He was ready to follow Larry, and he had learned to be a bit afraid of the city.

Larry had been going to the games for years and had a set route. He would walk down Bay Street, cross Van Ness, and catch the cable car at Hyde. The car would climb Russian Hill, and they would jump on the Number Ten Muni bus, which would drop them off at the corner of King and Third. Once off the bus, it was a short walk to the base of the fifth arch way in right field, which held the exclusive Dog Patch Clubhouse.

"The Patch," as it was known, held about one hundred dogs, and Sam came to learn that, like all small groups, there was a code to be followed. The good news for Sam was that Larry knew the code, and Sam was soon enough a member of the club, as everyone could see how much he loved the Giants.

Larry turned out to be a bit of a picky traveler. If anything was amiss in the schedule or if anyone made a small misstep, he was on it. The best way to describe it was that he was living his life in a constant state of disappointment. The tourists on the cable car, the kids on the muni, the smell of the bay in McCovey Cove – something was always not as good as it used to be, or there was reason for a lament. Sam, for his part, wasn't too worried about those things. He loved the Giants, he loved being a part of his family, and he loved being in the club at "the Patch."

For several years things didn't change much for Sam or the Giants. The years came and went. The team was good but lacked hitting, so they could never get to the World Series. Sam's routines were set, and he settled into the comfort that comes with certainty. However, in February San Francisco is a city in the midst of change, and in February 2010 the first of several changes knocked on Sam's door.

CHAPTER 2
Pitchers and Catchers Report

"People ask me what I do in the winter when there's no baseball. I'll tell you what I do. I stare out the window and wait for spring."
–RODGERS HORNSBY

February eighteenth 2010 was a date marked on every loyal Giants fan's calendar. Pitchers and catchers were to report to spring training. The reason they report early is because of the symbiotic bond that must be formed by these two positions on the field. They must be in sync on every pitch, or the game can get away quickly. The San Francisco Giants were coming into the 2010 season with a pitching staff stacked with young talent and a catching crew anchored by the confident but sensitive Bengie Molina.

Larry had been talking about two things all winter: the Giants needed to sign a big bat, and how fast their first round draft pick, Buster Posey, was going to replace Bengie Molina as catcher. On February eighteenth 2010, there was no new big bat in the lineup, and, while Buster was in spring training for the second consecutive year, it was still clear that Bengie was in control of the catching position. Change, it seemed, was far away for this team.

After coming home from his walk on Saturdays, Sam would sit near Larry's house, and they would listen to Marty Lurie talk about the possibilities of the New Year. "You never know" was Marty's tag line, and, while Sam thought that sounded accurate, Larry wasn't buying it. "Where are the runs going to come from," and "When is Buster showing up?" were his battle cries.

Another thing happened on February eighteenth 2010 that neither Sam, nor Larry for that matter, could quite understand. A large sign was posted on the door of Larry's flat. For two quick hours on a Sunday afternoon, almost one hundred strangers walked through Larry's flat. The strangers spoke with a person whom Sam thought smelled like prunes, but whom Larry said was in advertising because her face was on all the shopping carts at the Safeway. Larry and Sam had been regulated to their dog houses for the exercise, and the strange event was over just as soon as it began. Later that week, the stranger came back, and she was smiling from ear to ear. The only thing Sam couldn't quite figure out was that his owners didn't seem to be as excited as the stranger. Larry thought that his owners must be starting a new company and that this lady had just found them some space on a billboard downtown.

Neither dog was ready for what came next. On March twenty-fifth, the sign in the window came down, and a large moving truck appeared. All of the Larry's things were loaded up in that truck. Sam was in shock, and Larry, for a rare instance, could barely speak. Larry was moving to some place called Fresno, and he was leaving today. Sam couldn't believe it; he didn't understand it, and he certainly didn't like it. The movers took Larry's dog house away in seconds – radio and all. Before he could adjust his collar or scratch his ear, Larry was saying goodbye.

"Remember what I taught you, Sam. Stay close to the pack, stick to your routines, and don't explore the city. The Giants need you, Sam. Here is my pass to the "Dog Patch"; take good care of it. Goodbye."

With that, Larry turned and, in his trademark awkward way of walking, strode up to his owners' Audi SUV and waited to be picked up and put in the front seat.

Sam stood there watching the Audi SUV with the Giants' logo on the back windshield drive away. He repeated to himself, "Goodbye? Stay close to the pack?" What pack? Larry was his pack. "Stick to his routines?" Larry was involved with all his routines. "Don't explore the city?" That was easy; Sam didn't want to go anywhere. Worse yet, if The Giants needed him, that was great, but Sam's dog house didn't have a radio! Not knowing what else to do, Sam went into his Petco special doghouse that didn't smell like anything and started to chew on one of the corners.

CHAPTER 3

Getting Ready to Bounce

"What counts is not necessarily the size of the dog in the fight; it's the size of the fight in the dog."
– DWIGHT D. EISENHOWER

For ten straight days, Sam's new routine consisted of staying close to his family, realizing the new people who moved into Larry's flat did not have a dog, and working on that corner of his dog house as a way to deal with his frustration. It didn't taste like a stick or a sock. It actually had no taste at all, and every once in a while he would wonder to himself why he was chewing something he couldn't taste. However, that thought would pass, and he would go back to chewing.

On April third, Sam caught a break when his owners bought him a new dog house. He was elated to see that it was a larger version of Larry's Redwood palace. The new house came with the Giants' logo on the side, a place for Sam's name on the door, and it even smelled like AT&T

Park! Sam leaped and leaped; he ran in circles while it was put in place. And once he was inside, he noticed it had a radio! Sam was back! He could listen to the Giants! In a moment of sly humor, he said to himself, "Hmm...I am only going to have to listen to one conversation without Larry here – how simple!"

Once he had all his belongings in his new house, he also noticed a place for five dog tags that were inlaid into the redwood on the front wall. He didn't think much of it at the time, as he decided that something must have been missing in the packaging. To his continued delight, the Giants were starting the season on the road in Houston, and he could now follow along on his radio.

The home opener was just days away – April ninth, against the Atlanta Braves. Sam had to figure out how he was going to get to the game. Something inside him told him that he wasn't made for sitting on cable cars and Muni buses; he decided to switch things up and walk to the game. However, he still wasn't sure about his route. His plan was to follow the water from Ft. Mason all the way to the yard. That was the simplest route, but it also was the longest. He would keep it simple and talk to no one; he would be safe once he made it into "The Dog Patch." He went to sleep listening to the radio and dreaming about wild-man Jonathan Sanchez, who would be slinging it from the bump the next day.

CHAPTER 4
Opening Day

"You look forward to [Opening Day] like a
birthday party when you're a kid. You think
something wonderful is going to happen."
– JOE DIMAGGIO

Opening day in San Francisco is a celebration. Some cities celebrate opening day as the end of winter, and they rejoice that grass is growing (and hopefully less snow is falling). For San Francisco, there is no snow, and grass grows year round. For longtime city residents, spring is about the shift in winds and awaiting for the inland counties to heat up to draw the ocean fog across the avenues and through the golden gate like a freight train.

The history of the Giants and their ball parks began with a few short years at Seal Stadium. Then they quickly turned south, when the team put a round chalice of concrete on Candlestick Point, six miles south of downtown. There was no need for a dome, as the sun shines from May to November in Northern California. But at Candlestick

Point, the prodigious winds sweep up to the stadium like ghosts and then spill over the top. Once inside, the trailing forces of Mother Nature keep those winds trapped inside, and the imprisoned winds wreak havoc on all the souls inside. A baseball struck poorly will rise in the air with a variety of spin, and, for forty years, anyone who ever played at Candlestick will tell you that there was no such thing as an easy fly ball. The spectators were not spared either, as an ill fitted cap or unpinned hair-do stood no chance in the cauldron that was known as "The Stick."

On March thirty-first 2000, after years of public deliberation and subtle single issue group massaging, the Giants unveiled what was thought to be a hitter's paradise in Pac-Bell Park. A short five miles north and situated ten blocks south of Market Street, the new park was even closer to the water than Candlestick. With forty years of local knowledge under their belt and a few season ticket holders still looking for their favorite hats, the stadium architects needed to come up with a winning design. Their solution was to create a wedge for the wind to go around and over. The designers also gave the ghostly forces an exit pattern, as the outfield stands gave way to sweeping vistas of the Bay Bridge and the East Bay Hills.

From a baseball perspective, the thought was just to hit the ball really high so the wind would carry it out – after all, Barry Bonds was in his prime, and everyone loves a home run, right? Well, ten years later, everyone had learned that Barry was the only one who could hit the ball out, and even he seemed a bit over matched.

April ninth 2010 brought the Atlanta Braves to town to face a Giants team that had been hand crafted by General Manager Brian Sabean. The Giants in the post-Bonds era had invested heavily in young, strong pitchers who challenged hitters to battle the sky and wind. Whatever was left in owner Bill Neukom's pocketbook went to creative and crafty position players.

The fans and the city were abuzz for the mid-day start, and Sam awoke excited, and a bit afraid, for his first solo trip to the yard. As Sam left his house, he noticed Larry's pass to The Patch and decided he would bring it along out of memory. Hopefully, it might bring some good luck. With purpose and focus, Sam crossed Bay Street at the Octavia Street stoplight, scampered across the expanse of Fort Mason, and within minutes was next to his guide post for the day, the San Francisco Bay. Sam loved the smell of the water. It filled his black nose with a myriad of smells that went deep into his genetic code. He couldn't describe it, but the salt water made him feel alive.

Still, he had a schedule, and he resisted an urge to jump into the bay. Instead, he scampered along past Aquatic Park and made his way through Fisherman's Wharf and Pier Thirty-Nine. Sam remembered Larry's words about not talking to strangers and thought that not talking to people in this part of San Francisco was easy. None of them were from here, and they all had awkward looking attire and seemed to walk with no sense of purpose. It was as if they had nowhere to go and all day to get there.

South of Pier Thirty-Nine, Sam started to get a bit thirsty. He thought about finding a puddle and satisfying his need there, but each time his nose told him to beware. By the time he was next to the Pier Twenty-Three Grill, his tongue was starting to stick out from the side of his mouth. The excitement of opening day and the prolonged exercise was new to six year old Sam, and he was a bit out of shape for a lab. In fact, you could say he was "Pugish." Fortune smiled on Sam, as the Pier Twenty-Three Grill was owned by the dog-loving Flicka McGurrin, who always kept a water bowl out in front. Sam's nose gave it a big thumbs up.

Lapping up more water than normal, Sam decided to sit for a spell and catch his breath, which allowed him to become aware of his surroundings for the first time. He had such a focus on getting to the park, and the salt water had caused his senses to be on overload; he now found he was a bit gassed. Now with some fresh water in his tank and with the knowledge that he was more than half way to The Yard, he noticed a six year old golden retriever sipping a cappuccino. Without much provocation and before Sam could avert his eyes, the other dog said, "Good morning. You look a little spent."

Sam had really not wanted to talk to anyone. This was a big day, and he was doing so well at following Larry's laws. He would soon be safe at The Patch. Why had he looked at that dog? And why oh why had this total stranger said hello to him? Furthermore, how rude could one be? Even if Sam was spent, the retriever should not have pointed it out.

Still, Sam was a lab, and this guy looked like him a bit. His natural expression was so open that Sam heard himself say, "Well, I am off to opening day. I have an extra ticket; do you want to go with me?"

Sam's heart stopped the moment the words were out of his mouth. Had he really just asked a total stranger to The Patch? Would the guys at the club approve? He was confused. Why he had done that? Was it the new route? Was it the exercise? Was it the salt water in the air? Sam didn't know, but still there was the chance the golden would turn him down.

"Sure!" the golden said. "That sounds like an adventure. Let's get going."

Sam was now stuck with his unexplainable offer. He followed up the acceptance with a soft, "Oh, and my name is Sam."

"I'm Brad." The golden gleamed back at him. "Thanks for the invitation. I am in town from Portland for a few days, and we don't have a Major League club. This will be my first Big League game."

"Great," Sam thought, "I am honoring Larry's first missed game in ten years with a total rookie. And worse yet, he is from Oregon!"

Soon enough, the pair was clipping along together down the Embarcadero. Before they could get to the next pier, Brad was peppering Sam with questions.

"How long have you lived here? Are the Giants any good? Who is your favorite player? What do you do on Sundays? Do you know where I can get some good Chinese food?"

Sam was totally flustered. He didn't have answers to half the questions, and the other half were not at all appropriate for a stranger to be asking him.

"Ugh! My whole life, the Giants have needed to find a good batter. But they have a chance this year – Matt Cain. I go for a walk with my family on Sundays. And finally, I have never had Chinese food; I eat at home where it is safe."

Brad, for his part, didn't seem fazed at all by Sam's lackluster answers; he was extremely fit and seemed to notice things that Sam never would have seen by himself. He also seemed to view all interactions with others as a chance to listen, relate, and learn as much as he could from whomever he met. He also had a special tag on his collar with a red cross on it. He didn't bring it up, and Sam was still in so much shock that it could have been a hat on Brad's head and Sam would have missed it.

The other curious thing about this pair of dogs walking to the game was they were the same age, the same size, and both had noses that came alive when they were around the water. As they reached AT&T Park and Sam and Brad were admitted to The Patch, the game was just getting started. Ex-49ner great Steve Young was throwing a football to the great wide receiver, Jerry Rice. The crowd went wild.

Brad turned to Sam and said just loud enough so that the other dogs couldn't ignore him, "I thought we were going to watch a baseball game?"

Sam cringed and sank into his seat. How could he have been so foolish to invite this out of town rube into The

Patch? Sam had just learned all the secret non-spoken rules: no talking during an inning, only eat your food in the left side of your mouth, and, if you have to scratch or sniff yourself, you must go outside the club. Old dogs went first in the chow line, and, whatever you do, don't leave your collar on when you are inside. Now, within seconds of the game starting, Brad was talking like he was at a bar. Sam was sure he would get a letter from the membership committee.

The game itself was a thriller. The Giants won on an infield single in the bottom of the thirteenth inning by Aaron Rowand, who was safe via a head first dive. AT&T Park was in instant bedlam, and the team poured out onto the field, mobbing Rowand. The members of The Patch were more subdued; they smiled at each other and then filed out of the club. Most had cars waiting to take them to their next club for some drinks and a round or two of cards.

Brad had calmed down and watched the game with ease. He picked up on the rules (much to Sam's relief) and actually seemed to understand a lot of the game, almost from an intuitive state. Sam had hoped to say goodbye at the game, but Brad offered to buy him dinner as a thank you. He said he had learned about a great Chinese place in the Marina from another dog when he was out for one of his frequent scratch and sniff breaks.

As they walked home along the Embarcadero, Brad made his second observation of the day (his first had been to say Sam looked spent). In the interim, he had just been asking questions. Sam, for his part, had asked no questions or made any observations. The game and The Patch had been his safety blankets, and soon enough Sam would be back at home listening to the post game wrap up on KNBR.

Brad turned towards Sam and said, "Sam, if you don't my saying so, you appear to be a little stuck."

"Stuck? Stuck? What does he mean?" Sam thought. "I am not stuck. I am just following the rules that Larry set out for me. I am still getting used to not having Larry around here. What does he mean by stuck?"

Finally Sam said, "I don't know what you mean by stuck."

"Well, for one thing," Brad offered, "after asking me if I wanted to go the game with you, you didn't ask me another question. The game was a thrilling experience, but where we watched it was very antithetical to the game itself. We had all these rules that had no bearing on the game, and the crowd's emotion didn't seem to penetrate the club. I had to go scratch and sniff a few extra times just so I could catch the vibe. When I met you, you had a look in your eye of excitement and verve. But the moment we entered The Patch, that dog went away, and a different Sam was sitting next to me. So I thought I would see if you were stuck in between two places in life. You appear to know how to act one way, but I think your natural state – your chocolate Labrador retriever state – is looking to come out."

Sam was stunned. How on earth did this stranger know his past so well after just going to a baseball game with him? Sam hadn't even talked to him that much. He stopped, looked at Brad, and, for the second time that day, shared something he normally wouldn't.

"My mentor just moved away last week," said Sam, "and I am really lost as to what to do next. I had my life right where I thought I wanted it. Now that Larry is gone, I am not sure if I was living his life or mine. I mean, he is a pug and I am a lab. We are both dogs, but, after that, the similarities stop."

Brad smiled and gave Sam a head and body shiver to say, "I get it," and broke into a quick jog. Sam immediately joined him, and soon they were off running towards the Golden Gate Bridge. Both dogs ran with great ease, and, before Sam knew it, they were at Crissy Field.

While still running, Brad said, "Sam, I am down here in San Francisco doing some stand-up comedy with a troupe of actors. We study an art form called 'improv.' I would like to share with you the roots of our art form, as I think they might make some sense for you right now. They also might help you on your discovery of who you are. Do you mind if I share them?"

Sam, feeling a little spent again, said, "Sure, but do you mind if we stop running for a while?"

They had reached the Crissy Field warming hut and slowed to a walking pace along the water towards the base of the Golden Gate Bridge.

Brad continued, "Improv is about three principles, noticing more, letting go, and using everything."

Sam looked puzzled, but again the salt water had awakened a whole new part of his brain. He said, "I don't get it. Can you give me some examples?"

Brad smiled and said, "Today had several perfect examples of each. When you bounced into Pier Twenty-Three, I was reflecting about how our performance went last night. I was also fully aware of my surroundings because, as student of improv, everything and everyone is a potential prop in the pursuit of adventure."

Brad paused and looked at Sam to make sure the lab was keeping up. "Sam, I saw you from one hundred yards away. You cut a curious figure, and my immediate reaction was that you might be a member of the Water Dog Rescue Society."

Sam's ears perked up at this. "What is that?" he asked.

"The Water Dog Rescue Society is a volunteer group for dogs who love the water. They patrol bodies of water to protect humans and dogs alike. They are like dog lifeguards."

Sam guffawed at this. "Me, a dog lifeguard? The moment I get in the water, I end up smelling like the bay. Then I have an amazing urge to roll around in the nearest patch of dirt."

Brad chuckled. "Well, it does have some obstacles, but we typically have a shack or two where we clean up after a practice swim or a real rescue."

Sam stopped and stared at Brad. They now were at Fort Point, which sits next to the anchorage of the south end of the Golden Gate Bridge.

"You mean to tell me you are a Water Dog Rescue Society member?"

Again Brad smiled and said, "Yes. I wear this badge on my collar as a symbol to show that, if needed, I will jump in that water right there."

Sam then posed a question that meant he was catching up to where Brad was leading him. "But what does that have to do with improv?"

Brad peered out at the water that churned right beneath the Golden Gate. Then he looked squarely at Sam. "A rescue dog has a zeal for adventure in his soul. Improv is about looking at all conversations as an opportunity for adventure. The two go hand in hand."

Sam thought about the two concepts and was able to grasp the water part easier than the improv part. He always wanted to get in the water.

Being open and letting go were not things Larry had ever talked about, and this guy Brad was from Portland – what did he know? They didn't even have a Big League club! Still, it was pretty compelling to think about. So Sam replied, "Okay, I like the water dog part, but you said you had several examples from today about improv. What else?"

Brad turned to start their journey back to the Marina; they had been talking for so long that it was now too late for dinner. Instead, they agreed to walk back to Sam's house together.

Brad continued, "Today's game was an improv artist's dream. Could anyone have ever scripted that the game would go thirteen innings? That Barry Zito, a starting pitcher, might have been the next option for Bruce Bochy to use as a reliever? Who would have thought that Edgar Renteria would hit a game tying two run homerun in the top of the ninth and that the closer, Brian Wilson, would have to pitch to extend the game in the tenth? For the manager, this was either really hectic or just another night at the yard. My guess is that he is used to this, as baseball, for all its "certainty," is all about adapting and using everything around you to make do."

Sam was dumbfounded. How, in one day, could a total stranger completely blow up almost every paradigm and truth he had ever known? First off, Sam loved the water;

secondly, he actually enjoyed his walk to the park. He was enjoying talking to a stranger, and now he could see how baseball might not be as "by the book" as Larry had said. Just then, Sam realized that Larry had never played any sports at all.

Sam chuckled to himself as they walked by the local Safeway and could see his home up the street. Brad looked puzzled, and Sam explained.

"Brad, I have had quite a day, and I have a lot to think about thanks to you. I hope we can keep in touch, and you are welcome to come to a Giants game with me anytime."

Brad gave Sam a high five and then gave him a dog tag with his name on one side and some words inscribed on the other side. It said:

Brad said, "Read these aloud every day, and watch what happens. I hope these six words help you as you continue to find out who you are, Sam. Don't forget about the Water Dog Rescue Society! They have a great chapter down here, and I would be happy to connect you with the leadership if you have an interest. Thanks again for a great day."

Sam turned into his flat and found his doghouse a welcome home. He sat down, had a big slurp of water, and turned on the radio. KNBR was still abuzz over the win. The callers were mostly gushing over the day itself and the chances of the team. There was the odd naysayer speaking of the need for some speed and the overall age of the team, but even the gloomiest fan would have to agree that the home opener had been a smash hit.

Sam thought about Larry and how he must have missed being at the park. He knew that, somewhere in the central valley, Larry was listening. "I bet he was really worried about Brian Wilson pitching in the tenth today. I wonder what "The book" says about that."

CHAPTER 5

Building Momentum Out of the All Star Break

*"Our job as coaches is to love you. Your
job as players is to love each other."*
– Joe Ehrmann

The two months that transpired between opening day and June thirtieth saw the city of San Francisco slip into its summer weather pattern of fog, wind, and cool, moist air. The Giants almost let their season slip away, and Sam was sticking to most of what Larry had told him, except for a few changes.

He had stayed a vigilant follower of the road games on the radio, and he had attended every home game. He was a regular at The Patch, following the rules and deciding against bringing guests after his time with Brad. He did, however, walk to the games, and, almost as if Larry had taught him, he went the same way every time. He loved walking along the waterfront. He smiled at strangers but didn't invite them to the games, and he hadn't seen Brad.

The walking, along with his recent trial membership in the San Francisco chapter of the WDRS, had him down ten pounds, and his coat was as shinny as ever. In the two months, Sam had taken Brad's encouragement to say aloud his six words. After the awkward first few times, he enjoyed the act of repeating them each day. Was Sam a little different? Yes. Was he a Labrador retriever in full? No.

June thirtieth was a pivot point for the Giants, as they left for Colorado heading in the wrong direction. The weak western division notwithstanding, being swept by the Dodgers at AT&T Park did not sit well with anyone. To add to the frustration, the Giants had their first losing home streak of the year. With a record of 40 and 37, the momentum machine was missing for this team. And before the team plane landed in Colorado, General Manager Brian Sabean made a move.

As news that Bengie Molina had been traded to the Texas Rangers reached Sam's doghouse, he smiled and thought, "Well, Larry is getting one of his wishes for the season. They are calling up the kid." Buster Posey was that kid, and he would spark a fire in the team that would lead to him being named the July Major League player of the month in his first full month in the big leagues.

The team stayed on the road and headed into the All-Star break on the cusp of turning the season around. They opened up the second half of the year at home on July fifteenth against the New York Mets. Sam could hardly wait to get out the door. Lincecum was on the mound, and, because he had not been used in the All-Star game, he was fresh.

CHANGE DOESN'T BITE

Sam was ready for another exciting day at The Yard. He popped down to the waterfront, which was becoming a second home for him now. He was right in the middle of Fisherman's Wharf when he was diverted by some new construction on the Embarcadero. Sam noticed an alleyway that directed him back to Bay Street. Bay Street was part of his old route with Larry to the Hyde Street cable car. Sam thought about saying hi to the cable car drivers, but Columbus Street was calling him with its angular and direct route to the park.

No sooner was he on Columbus then he was in what is known as the North Beach district of San Francisco. The cafés that lined Columbus Avenue were a testament to the profits one could make selling ground coffee beans. Sam was navigating the hill nicely in his svelte state, but he was a little thirsty. He noticed a dog bowl at David Wright's "Café Divine," which sat next to Washington Square Park. He went over for a fill-up and to take in his new surroundings. Washington Park was to the west, and on its northwest corner stood St. Peter and Paul Church. The east side of the park housed Moose's restaurant and the Italian Athletic club. Sam's gaze turned back to the bowl, and he was about to take another series of slurps when an extremely large and intimidating Rottweiler appeared and politely asked, "Is this your first time to Washington Park?"

Sam was taken aback by a few things. The first was the insightfulness of the question; the second was the softness with which the large dog spoke. He looked up to take in the full measurements of the black and tan canine and noticed the softest eyes he had ever seen amidst a relaxed face. The rest of this animal shouted brute force and stay away, but not the face.

"Actually it is," Sam remarked. "I have lived in the Marina my whole life but have never seen this park before today. It smells great."

The Rottweiler said, "I thought so; you took in the whole area with the gaze of a stranger. My name is Joe. What's yours?"

"I am Sam."

"Well Sam, what are you doing in North Beach? If I may say, you look like you have been moving at a pretty fast clip to get here by the way you were drinking from that water bowl."

Sam took a long look at Joe while he pondered the question. The exterior of this dog made it hard to not take any question the wrong way. However, his voice was soft, and his words came out smoothly. In light of the positive expression and the tone of the question, Sam let go of the "stranger" caution flag in his mind and shared freely with Joe.

"I am on my way to see Lincecum pitch against the Mets. The Giants are starting to turn it around, and the new kid, Posey, appears to have provided a real spark to the team."

Joe lit up when Sam spoke of the Giants. "A Giant's game? That is great; you seem to really follow the team closely."

"Well," Sam demurred, "my old mentor – or neighbor I should say – was a diehard fan, and I picked it up over the years."

Joe said, "Any way you can get into the game is fine with me, just as long as you love it and understand why you love it. Tell me more about your neighbor. He seems like an interesting fellow."

Sam thought of the time and his schedule as he pondered how to share his thoughts on Larry with Joe fairly but with brevity. He did want to get to the game, but he also wanted to share what he had been learning with Joe. The extra pass to the game crossed his mind – that would give him them plenty of time. He thought of Brad and the stress of bringing a guest into The Patch. He wasn't sure that Joe was the "take your collar off when indoors" type. Still, the words on the front of his dog house were milling around in his mind, and he offered.

"Well Joe, that is a bit of a story, and I happen to have an extra ticket to today's game. Would you like to join me?"

Joe sprang up from his spot on the curb with surprising ease and shook his collar a bit. "A Giants game! Are you kidding me? I would love to go! I know a great way to the park."

With that, they were off towards downtown on Columbus Avenue. They went through downtown on Montgomery Street across Market Street. As Montgomery Street turned into First Street, they started to go west a block or two to get to Third Street. During this time, Sam shared with Joe all about his life and about how he had met Larry and what he had learned. Joe was a great listener, and Sam just talked and talked. So much had been changing for him, and he had been experiencing it mostly on his own. Having Joe as a sounding board felt great.

They weaved their way through the large blocks that were south of Market Street. Sam noticed that, as they passed dogs who were near a restaurant or bar, they said hello to Joe. Joe would return the salutation and, in almost every case, called the other dog by its name. Sam found this a bit odd, as they were now quite a ways from North Beach.

"Joe, how is it that you know all these dogs?"

"I have been around for a long time. San Francisco is my home. If I had to guess, I have been in every neighborhood or district this seven-by-seven city has."

Sam knew that San Francisco was essentially a seven mile square at the top of a peninsula, but what Sam found amazing was that, in his own six years, he had covered less than seven blocks. Besides the route to AT&T Park and The Patch, Sam had seen very little of San Francisco.

"What took you to all these places?" Sam asked.

"Sports and faith," Joe replied.

Puzzled, Sam prodded, "What do you mean?"

Joe responded, "I was brought up in the Western Addition. At an early age, I found that my size and speed allowed me to excel at any physical competition. Soon enough, I was competing for a local club, and we had matches in every neighborhood. Those days were full of fighting and frustration for me, as I had a very difficult upbringing. Later in life, I became a minister, and I have been going back around the city working with puppies and their parents on how to help raise a generation of dogs that will lead this city into the future. My home church is in North Beach, but I view all of San Francisco as my home"

Sam felt his head inch up a bit as he thought of the celebrity he was now walking with to the game. Sam immediately wanted to be his best just because he had met Joe. Just as that thought passed, his next thought was of The Patch. He would be bringing a celebrity, and he was sure some of the old dogs there would know Joe.

Sam turned to Joe and said, "Joe, something I haven't mentioned is that my extra ticket is to an exclusive club for only one hundred dogs called The Patch. We sit just under the fifth archway in right field. It has catered food and is quite exclusive. I am sure you have heard of it."

Joe kept walking but slowed a bit. "I know The Patch. It's a nice place; I've been to a game there with the mayor's dog once. But if you don't mind, I have a different place I prefer to watch the game from."

A bit stunned Sam said, "Oh, does it have room for me too?"

"Of course it does," Joe bellowed. "I am excited to take in the game with you. I had planned on surprising you and an old buddy of mine at the game."

Relieved and now in a small amount of shock, Sam found his pace had quickened.

"But keep it nice and slow," Joe mentioned. "I have a few nagging old injuries, and I can't keep up with you labs. You guys are natural land and sea all-stars."

Sam noticed the mention of the sea and thought about bringing up his Water Dog Rescue Society training, but he kept it inside. Joe was so humble that the thought of bragging to him made no sense. They were soon at Second and King Street intersection. With Joe leading the way, they went around the Orlando Cepeda statue and headed toward the players' entrance. A security guard saw them coming and had the gate open by the time they arrived.

"How you doing, Joe?" came the greeting.

"Pretty good, Jerry, pretty good. I have a companion with me today if you don't mind."

"Not a problem at all. I am sure Chief will welcome the company," replied Jerry, and he gave Sam a knowing wink, like he knew that Sam was in for a treat.

AT&T Park, like any large sporting structure, has several worlds mixed together on game day. The players, the public, the vendors, and the peace keepers all have to be able to function. Most people will only ever see the park from the perspective of a ticket holder, and even the players have a narrow view of the facility. For the vendors and the peace keepers, the facility is a workplace and a show all at the same time. The game cannot be interrupted, and the fans need to have their experience. Most of this happens with meticulous planning and vigilant follow up by the hundreds of vendors and the San Francisco Police.

The centerfield scoreboard at AT&T Park holds one of the largest video screens in the region and, by itself, is seven stories tall. The fans stare at it to understand a multitude of things. But what they don't know is that within the structure sits a bank of screens and several members of the SFPD who are looking back at all of them!

As Joe and Sam navigated their way through the inside of AT&T Park, Sam couldn't quite catch his breath. Who had he stumbled upon in North Beach, the Pope? He had been a fan of the Giants for five years and a member of The Patch for three, but never in his wildest dreams could he have thought of being in the tower at AT&T Park. They had to get through several security guards, and all had the same reaction as Jerry, a salutation to Joe and a wink to Sam.

The police command center was their destination, and, once inside, it was cozy, but for Sam it was amazing. Joe introduced Sam to Chief, who was a medium sized eight year old mutt whom Joe had mentored seven years ago when Chief was orphaned. Turns out, Chief had lived with Joe for a few months as he was getting his life put together. Now six years into the San Francisco Police Force, Chief gave Joe a big hug and gave Sam his paw.

"If you're with Joe, then you're good by me" he said. "Welcome to the command center."

Sam was speechless and thought briefly about mentioning that he was a member of The Patch. But he thought better of it when he saw that one of the screens had a nice view of The Patch's dining room on display.

"Nice to meet you as well, sir," Sam muttered.

"Sir?" Chief chuckled. "No need for that around here. Just enjoy the game, and, if Joe gives you a pointer or two, I would write it on a wall and repeat it to myself every day." As he said this he gave Joe a nod.

Now it was Joe's turn to chuckle. "Funny how some of that self-talk magic sticks with you, isn't it Chief?"

Sam, feeling a bit on the outside of a very close relationship, laughed along, but he didn't really know why. Joe was quick to turn his attention back to his guest, and he showed Sam the best place to watch a game, "The Tower."

Tim Lincecum pitched a complete game shutout to lead the Giants to a two to zero win. He needed only one hundred ten pitches to dispatch the Metropolitans of New York, and the game was over in a brief two hours and eleven minutes. From Sam's perspective, the game was a blur. He was in the Tower; Joe and he had continued to talk about life, and the police had more activity than he thought made sense. However, Chief said it was just another night at the yard.

"Any time you get this many people together, things are bound to happen," was Chief's retort.

Sam and Joe filed out of the stadium and said good bye to all the people Sam had met. The dogs' dialogue went back to Sam and his recent changes. Joe and Sam walked home along the Embarcadero wall until they came to Broadway, at which point they took a left and climbed their way up to

North Beach. Along the way, Joe started sharing his thoughts on his favorite subject, coaching.

"We are all coaches. We start by coaching ourselves with our thoughts and our self-talk. The dialogue you have having with yourself has a huge impact on the life you lead and how you relate to others. For many, life is a series of trips from home plate to first base, as they battle all the bad things that have happened. They keep reliving them over and over again with their self-talk. In the baseball metaphor, they never round first and move on to advance in the game of life. Creating a heart and mind that can have empathy for those who have harmed you is a major enabler when it comes to rounding first in your life."

Sam thought about what Joe was sharing and was very thankful for his family life growing up. Even though Larry's coaching may have not been perfect, at least he had a mentor.

Joe continued, "The first word that I want to leave you with today is 'empathy.' When you have found the way to be empathetic towards all the people you have interacted with and can see their actions within the context of what they were struggling with while they were interacting with you, you will have mastered empathy.

"The second thing that is important to incorporate into your life is an attitude of being 'others focused.' Having empathy and being 'others focused' go hand in hand and make for great tools for having wonderful relationships."

Sam inserted, "You know this is right in line with what I was telling you on the way to the game about Brad the golden retriever and the study of improv. When you are open to change and have an adventurous spirit, you notice more. The moment you notice more, you meet more people. And the moment you meet more people, you have an opportunity to be a curious listener and seek to understand how they feel."

Joe smiled from ear to ear as they turned on Columbus Street and were coming close to Washington Square Park. "Sam, I am so happy this is making sense to you. I believe you are in a strong position to really make a difference in this city as you start to develop your skill sets."

Joe stopped as they made it back to Café Divine. "Sam, I have a final charge for you, and it is this: The dogs like you, who are able and strong, are needed by those that are less fortunate. I want you to find the cause greater than yourself that will benefit from your talents."

Sam paused and thought aloud, "I don't know what that is."

Joe responded, "It goes back to what I said when we met this afternoon: it is about your 'why.' Once your 'why' is in place, you can conquer any how."

With that, Joe gave Sam a dog tag that favored the one Brad had given him. It read:

I listen to others
I am others focused
I am passionate about my cause

"Sam, I want you to read these three affirmations every day out loud and then watch how your life begins to change. I also want you to explore this city, as it has so much to offer. If you ever get in a pinch, just mention my name or Chief's name, and you will be safe. In the process of exploring, you just might find your why."

Sam had listened to every word that Joe had said. With his new charge in his mind and his affirmations in his paw, he gave Joe a big hug.

"Thanks for saying hi today, Joe. Being with you was a real treat. I will work on my why and hope to share it with you someday soon."

"That sounds like a plan to me. I know you have what it takes." And with that, Joe went across the park to the cathedral, saying hi to what seemed like the entire population of the park.

Sam picked up the pace down Columbus, turned left on Bay Street, and was home in minutes. Back in his doghouse and with the post-game wrap in the background, Sam placed his new tag into the front wall.

July fifteenth had been a big day for the Giants, as they stood at 48 and 41 with less than half the year remaining. They were just starting to click. Sam felt as if his personal world was also clicking into place, as he blended Brad's and Joe's teachings into the following:

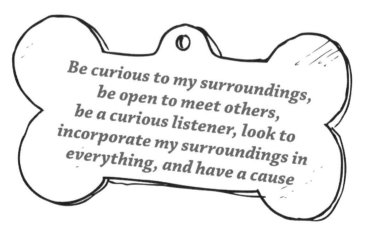

Be curious to my surroundings, be open to meet others, be a curious listener, look to incorporate my surroundings in everything, and have a cause

The last one nagged at him for a while. What was his cause?

CHAPTER 6
Clinching the Division

"Greatness and nearsightedness are incompatible.
Meaningful achievement depends on lifting one's
sights and pushing toward the horizon."
- Daniel H. Pink

San Francisco has weather that, for some, can be toxically cold and, for others, can be blissfully consistent. Most of the residents do not have air conditioning systems in their homes, as the proximity to the Pacific Ocean to the west and the bay to the east keeps the weather in a tight range. Old timers will tell anyone who will listen that the ocean is far larger than the landmass; thus, the temperature of the water matters much more than the temperature of the air. The Pacific Ocean, at latitude 37.7750, has an average water temperature of fifty-six degrees and stays close to that temperature year round.

CHANGE DOESN'T BITE

If San Francisco has a warm season, it is the fall. At this time, the fog can be gone, and so can the wind. When this happens, downtown heats up in a hurry, and city residents will open every available window. October 3, 2010 was one of these days, and, as the windows of the city opened, nearly every opening seemed to have some form of Giants sign hanging from the window sill.

"Let's go Giants," "Panda Mania," and "Fear the Beard" were just some of the slogans that had emerged. San Francisco was abuzz with what had been a good old-fashioned pennant race with the San Diego Padres. Jonathan Sanchez had added some spice by claiming that the Giants would catch the Padres in July. On the final day of the season, with none other than Sanchez on the mound, the Giants could clinch the division with a win over the Padres. The 1:05 p.m. start time assured that very little work would be accomplished, and AT&T Park was awash sunshine.

Sam had spent the last seventy-five days following every step of the season, working with his cause (the Water Dog Rescue Society chapter), and exploring San Francisco for the first time. Golden Gate Park, the Presidio, Ocean Beach, and the Mission had all been part of his training. Brad and Joe had been spot on with their assessments of how much San Francisco had to offer. San Francisco seemed to have fifty different ecosystems of weather, people, and dogs. Sam found it quite easy to assimilate in every environment, as he practiced his natural Labrador characteristics of openness, good humor, and affability. It also helped that he was providing a community service, and, when in doubt, he would bring up the Giants.

October 3, 2010 found Sam to be fit, focused, and fired up for the Giants to clinch the division. He had a busy day planned: a trip to the veterinarian took him south of The Yard to the UCSF Mission Bay campus, and, from there, it was a short jog north to the game.

As Sam left his appointment, he stopped at the UCSF Café for a quick drink of water. Sitting just inside the line of shade made by an awning and within close proximity to the water bowl was an odd looking pair of dogs. One was a white standard poodle; the other was a bull dog. They appeared to be in deep conversation on a topic, and Sam wondered if it might even be an argument.

With quite a bit on his mind and not looking to get pulled into a debate, Sam moved with purpose towards the bowl for his sustenance. No sooner had he taken his first slurp then the poodle turned to him and said, "Excuse me, my colleague and I are in the midst of a discussion. I hope you won't mind, but would you help us settle a dispute?"

"Dispute?" Sam remarked. "I am not qualified for dispute resolution. You might want to ask a Doberman or a collie."

"Nonsense," said the bulldog with a thick but educated British accent. "As a lab, you are more than qualified. Plus this is about all dogs, so lend us your ear."

Sam thought about lending someone his ear for a second and, with a mind towards his schedule, decided he could speak with this odd couple for a few minutes before setting off to the park.

"Okay," Sam said. "What is your quandary?"

"Well," the poodle remarked, "it is a simple question about motivation really."

"Nonsense," the bulldog retorted. "There is nothing simple at all about motivation. Dr. Csikszentmihaly's work proves that it is a complicated endeavor."

Sam shook his head briefly to make sure he had understood the name he had just heard. Dr. Who? And what work were they talking about with respects to motivation? Sam knew he was motivated to get to the game, and, the longer he was here, the less chance he had of seeing Sanchez pitch.

The poodle continued, "Yes, Ken, it is not 'simple,' but the question is this: how is the world going to educate its people in a way that is in line with our modern economy's market realities?"

Sam blinked. Who were these guys? Sam was worried about the playoff roster, Lincecum's velocity on his fastball, and the Panda's weight problem. The world economy and the education system didn't quite hit his radar screen.

"Um, excuse me, I am on my way to the Giants game, and I don't think I am the right guy for your discussion," Sam said with his best and softest tone.

"Giants game?" the bulldog exclaimed. "Is that going on today? I have always wanted to take in the American game of baseball. Is the club still owned by Bill Neukom and Peter Magowan?"

"Yes it is," Sam replied.

The bulldog turned to the poodle. "Well Daniel, let's pop over for a visit and continue our discussion while watching the young lads throw the ball around."

Sam chuckled. "This game is completely sold out, and the scalpers are getting five hundred dollars a ticket on the street."

Ken grimaced and remarked, "I don't need a ticket, and I certainly am not going to pay five hundred dollars in the after-market either. We will just go down and check in with Bill's German shepherd."

As they started walking towards the park, Sam couldn't help but be amazed by the thought of these two getting into the game. He had his extra pass to The Patch, but that would only help out one of them, and he wasn't even sure he wanted to share the experience of this game with either one of them. They also were not moving at a very fast pace, as the bulldog had a limp in his gate that he had picked up in a "war" in his majesty's service.

Sam's different route to the game had once again caused him to meet these very unique dogs, and it appeared he would be with them at least up to the park. Who knew after that?

"My name is Sam, by the way."

The poodle responded, "Mine is Daniel, but I go by D.P., and this is Sir Ken. We are in town lecturing at UCSF on the future of education. I am in from D.C., and, as you can tell, Ken is from London.

"I just moved to L.A., and everybody talks nonstop about the Dodgers," Ken snorted, while being a bit out of breath after about five blocks. "Can't make out what all the fuss is about. I prefer football, which is what you Yanks call soccer."

Sam bristled a bit with the mention of the Dodgers and found Ken's attitude a little caustic, but D.P. was smooth.

The last three hundred yards south of AT&T Park included a walk across the Lefty O'Doul Bridge. The bridge was full of fans, and energy was in the air. Sam, D.P., and Sir Ken made their way up to the executive offices. Once inside, the bulldog had a quick conversation with the security guard. In less than ten minutes, a German shepherd with an ascot of bright orange appeared; he was grinning from ear to ear.

"Sir Ken," he exclaimed. "What a surprise! You are here on one of the best days of the year. I am sure you will find the entire competition useful for your studies."

"I have two guests: my colleague Dan and our new friend, Sam, who appears to be a die-hard fan."

Sam muttered quickly, "Hello, I am a member of The Patch. I was going to the game already and met them at UCSF."

The German shepherd looked at Sam with a grace in his eyes that comes with privilege. He said, "That is wonderful. You have bumped into two of the world's leading thought leaders on motivation."

He turned to Ken. "I am chalk full at the moment Sir Ken. All the way up to my own luxury box. The fire marshal is running around here with his clip board and is threatening me with bad stats every fifteen minutes. However, I do have couple of spots in our dugout. I think this will allow you to get a good view of what the players are doing and experiencing during the game. All three of you can watch from there."

He turned to Sam and asked, "Do you think you would like to join them or watch from The Patch?"

Sam's look was of sheer astonishment. Had he just been invited into The Giants' dugout during the last game of the season? Was anyone not on the team ever in the dugout? Who had he just met, and how on earth was Sam going to keep his composure?

"The dugout would be great," Sam muttered.

"Splendid! By the way, my name is Keith."

Within in minutes, they were deep with the Park, walking through a tunnel that led to the holiest of locations – the home team dugout. The smells were fantastic to Sam; he smelled sweat, sunflower seeds, tobacco, and a new aroma he hadn't smelled before. D.P. told him the smell came from a cream used on sore muscles. And after one hundred sixty-one games, there were plenty!

Keith left the three dogs to themselves and returned to his other guests, promising to check in during the game. Sam, D.P., and Sir Ken settled in and watched the Giants take the field. The crowd roared, and Sam felt every hair on his body move from the energy. In all his years as a fan, he had never felt the emotion of the crowd from the ground level or felt so connected to the game.

D.P. and Sir Ken were smiling as well, but, to an observer, it was obvious they were looking at the event in a different light. Sam was a fan in the game; they were archeologists studying a living ecosystem. Sam saw Sanchez taking the mound to pitch against the struggling Padres and knew the drama that existed behind the scenes. It had been Sanchez who had predicted in July that the Padres would fold down the stretch. The media, always looking for a misspoken word to blow out of proportion, seized their opportunity, and, within hours, an extra layer of intrigue was in the air. Sanchez had eaten his words the next time he had taken the mound against San Diego. However, on October 3, 2010, his statement had come true, and the Giants were surging.

Sam knew the back story; he had listened to every talk show and was glued to the dynamic between Sanchez and every Padres batter. From his vantage point, drama and conflict were present in every bead of sweat the players brushed from their foreheads.

D.P. was looking at the team, but he noticed how connected they were and how much chemistry existed between the Giants players. His commentaries typically focused on how groups of people work well together. He spoke about words like "flow" and "momentum." He spoke to teenagers and to adults, and he felt that the demographics of America were such that people should pay attention to these topics to achieve their personal and team goals.

Sir Ken watched the team's fielding units interact. He saw a three layered system. The first line of defense was the pitcher and catcher. The second was the infield unit. The last was the trio of outfielders. He watched how they warmed up together and how they communicated on every pitch. Sir

Ken was a product of a large system himself, which was the United Kingdom. He, like all his countrymen, was a product of a country that had ruled the world through a system. Born at the tail end of that system's dominance but still educated by it, he had traveled the world writing and speaking about education. Witty by nature, and gruff or blunt to those who couldn't keep up, Sir Ken had a huge heart and was focused on helping people discover where they were intelligent. He also believed that, regardless of your area of natural talent, focused and diligent practice was necessary for achievement. Sir Ken was an optimist.

The three dogs were treated to quite the experience, as Sanchez pitched five solid innings of shutout baseball. He also got the Giants' offense going with a triple in the fifth inning and scored the game's first – and what turned out to be game winning – run. The Giants' bullpen kept the Padres at bay for the final four innings, and Brian Wilson's perfect ninth inning secured the Giants' three-zero victory. It was their first pennant in seven years!

The players stormed the field, the fans went nuts, and Pat Burrell and Aubrey Huff led a parade of Giants around the field to thank the fans. Forty-five thousand people didn't move, as actors and critics came together to celebrate. Sam, D.P., and Sir Ken were caught up in the moment and ended up in the locker room. It was the first time Sam had ever been soaking wet from something other than water. D.P. and Sir Ken were excited as well, both from a scientific nature and as fans of the sport. The energy of the moment had all three of them feeling fantastic.

As often happens after a life moment occurs, the strangers became best friends. For Sam and his out of town guests, the game turned into a celebration, which flowed out of the stadium and onto the streets of San Francisco. Bars and restaurants all over the city were filling up as fans shared their joy. Sam told D.P. and Ken that, as out-of-towners, he would take them to a local restaurant in the Marina that was very small and didn't take reservations (in fact, it didn't even have a sign).

They caught a cab and turned up at the corner of Greenwich and Buchanan Street, Which, from the naked eye, looks like any other corner in the Cow Hollow district of the city. Most of the restaurants were two blocks south on Union Street, and all you could see (other than three story homes and apartments) was a frame store across the street.

"I thought you said we were going to dinner," Ken said.

"We are," Sam replied. "Let's turn in here." He pointed to a corner door on the southeast edge of the intersection.

"This is one of the gems of San Francisco; it's called The Brazen Head."

Once inside, they were greeted by a smiling hostess, a dimly light room, and wonderful aromas of vegetables, spices, and meats. They were soon seated at one of the only fifteen tables that were nestled in and around a centrally located bar, which still had a TV showing the postgame show.

Sam remarked to his two guests as they sat at the table, "This is such a big day for the Giants. Who would have thought that my trip to the vet would have led me to the Giants' dugout with the two of you? Brad sure was right about letting go and noticing more."

D.P. asked, "Who is Brad, and what did he mean by 'letting go'?"

Sam shared a bit about how 2010 had been a year of great change for him, starting out with Larry moving, Sam taking a different route to the game, and his few encounters with Brad and Joe. He shared how he had joined the WDRS and had been enjoying San Francisco. He told them how he couldn't believe that he had experienced so little of the city in his first five years.

"That is fantastic, Sam," Sir Ken remarked. "The journey you are on this year is a great example of what D.P. and I are focusing on with our work. In the process of following your nose to the water that first day, you have found a few people who have assisted you in pursing your talents and in serving others."

D.P. added, "What we would add to that is that all individuals should ask themselves how and where they are intelligent. This question is vital for everyone to consider because it forces people to realize that they are intelligent somewhere."

Sir Ken added, "Everyone has a knack for something, and that correlates back to where that person is intelligent. In your case, Sam, it appears you have a knack for the water and for helping others – that is a great combination."

Sam knew that, if these two were important enough to get him into the dugout for the last game of the season, they knew what they were talking about. He had never thought about asking where or how he was intelligent. He also was pleased to hear that Sir Ken thought he was using his gifts with the Water Dog Rescue Society.

Continuing, Sir Ken said, "The trick is that, once you have your gifts identified, you need to practice and build upon those gifts. This is where work ethic comes into play, which gets us back to our earlier discussion on motivation."

"Well, we certainly don't need to go back to that right now," D. P. remarked. He continued, "Peak individual performance can be tied back to diligent practice time and time again. How to practice, what to practice, when to practice, and with whom to practice are all good questions. But the big question that we study is 'why' someone chooses to practice. We study people at different stages of ability in all aspects of life. We study people alone and in conjunction with others. That is why a game like today is so fascinating to us both, personally but also professionally. The Giants' players and coaches are a fifty person unit working together, but they are also working by themselves. They have a 'collective why' and a 'personal why.' Quite frankly, when they are playing baseball, they aren't worried about that at all, but we are. We study them to share with others how the rest of our society can train and build cohesive human systems into the future."

"Wow," Sam said. "That is a lot for me to process."

"Well," Ken added, "that is why they keep us in our academic houses most of the time. But we really do love watching teams compete."

D.P. added, "We love watching how they get into a state of flow, and everyone can recognize when the momentum has shifted in a sporting event."

Something in Sam's head clicked at that moment. "You mean like when Sanchez hit the triple and it energized the entire team?"

"Exactly! But it wasn't just the triple; it was who hit the triple. It also has a lot to do with how close the team is prior to the competition. The more interconnected a team is to each other, the more they feed off of each other. This is why, in team sports, the underdogs can win if they are a more cohesive unit."

Sam thought back to the acrimony of the Barry Bonds' years and how much friction was around those teams. Could there be a bit of truth to what his new friends were saying? He also thought about how close all the teams were when it came to talent, and he thought about what he was learning from the Water Dog Rescue Society training. The Society talked about swim buddies and trusting your teammates at all times.

Sanchez was the teammate who "called out" the team and stood up for them at the same time. His efforts contributed to the amazing chemistry in the dugout today, and his hit lifted all of them in an instant. Sam was quite amped by his new perspective on his favorite team and started to look into the future.

"Wow, I can't wait to see how they perform next week against the Atlanta Braves," he said.

The dinner continued with the three of them discussing the Giants' game and how so many different aspects of the game related to the work of D.P. and Sir Ken. When Sam called them a cab to take them back to their hotel and prepared to walk a few short blocks back to his flat, D.P.

turned to him and said, "Sam, we can't thank you enough for your hospitality and letting us accompany you to the game today."

"The pleasure was all mine," Sam said. "Watching the game from the dugout was a once in a lifetime experience for me. In addition, the two of you have changed how I will watch baseball for the rest of my life."

Sir Ken gave Sam his dog tag that had his contact information on it on one side. On the other side, it had four lines of text.

"Here you go Sam," said Sir Ken. "If you are ever in L.A., come by and say hi. I will take you to a football match and show you what real athletes look like!" He winked as he said the last part.

The cab drove off up Buchanan Street, and Sam looked at the tag and the lines of text. He knew right away where the new tag was going – the front of his doghouse had the perfect spot. He looked at the tag, and it read:

Sam smiled and broke into a brisk gate towards his home, thinking about what a day it had been. The Giants had won, and he had seen it all from the dugout. He thought back to Larry and his rules for a brief moment. Not talking to strangers was good advice for a pug, he decided, but not for a chocolate lab. Still, somewhere in Fresno Sam's old friend must be smiling from ear to ear – the Giants were Western Division Champs!

CHAPTER 7
Playoffs

*"Success comes from knowing that you did your best
to become the best that you are capable of becoming."*
- JOHN WOODEN

Sam awoke on Tuesday, October nineteenth with a great deal of expectation. His life had been extremely active since the Giants clinched the division. His duties with the WDRS had been full of live water rescue simulations, and Sam had excelled in the toughest of areas – the single solo retrieve. The water felt great each time he leapt into it, and his fur seemed made for the temperatures of the bay. He loved working in teams to retrieve from the bay, but, for some reason, he had a knack for the difficult solo retrieve. The trick was to stay in control while still having a soft grip on the drowning person's upper garment of clothing.

Sam also was so strong and broad shouldered that he could convey to the drowning person a sense of calm that was extremely necessary in a water rescue situation. Sam took his natural ability and followed the words and teachings of Sir Ken. He put in plenty of hours, and Sir Ken was right – when he practiced, his love for the activity made time evaporate.

In addition to his efforts with the Water Dog Rescue Society unit, his beloved Giants had beaten the Atlanta Braves in five games and had split the first two games with the dreaded Phillies in Philadelphia. Today was a day game with Matt Cain on the hill, and the Giants were hosting the next three games at AT&T Park. The Phillies were the pride of the National League and had plenty of solid hitters to go with the vaunted pitching staff. The East Coast biased media didn't give the Giants a chance, even though it was well understood that the Giants' pitching staff was excellent.

"They just don't score any runs," was the cry. "Can Cody Ross – the guy who wanted to be a rodeo clown – really outperform two series in a row?"

Splitting the road games had been a big deal for the Giants, yet the Giants knew that every game in San Francisco was crucial. If they had to head back to Philadelphia for games six and seven needing two wins, it would be difficult.

Sam had a busy morning, as his Water Dog Rescue Society work had him up on Nob Hill. They were doing a community service project in the park across the street from Grace Cathedral. He was happy it ended at ten a.m. because he wanted to watch radio host Mary Lurie broadcast live from in front of the ballpark. The scene around the ballpark on game day had become fantastic in the last two weeks, and Sam was pumped.

On his way up to Nob Hill in the morning, he had passed a café and noticed they sold biscuits. He made a mental note to drop back by there on the way down the hill to the game. The Nob Hill Café was owned by Michael Deeb and served its well-heeled clientele a mixture of California cuisine and light pastries. Sam jogged up Taylor Street and went in to the café to order two biscuits to go. The café had just opened, and, aside from the three employees, only one elderly patron was present. Sitting next to the man was a sleek, grey, elderly whippet.

The whippet sat next to the water bowl, and, as Sam went down for a drink, he noticed a smooth and worn gold SF Giants logo on his weathered collar. At the beginning of the Giants season, Sam would have hardly noticed the whippet at all because strangers were to be ignored. Now, just five months later, Sam noticed quite a lot. The whippet, for his part, had noticed Sam from half a block away. He had been impressed by how fit the young lab was and how well he expressed himself to the café staff.

The two dogs were naturally drawn to each other by proximity, by a lack of others around, and by each of their own awareness. To not talk to each other would have been almost impossible.

Sam started first. "That is a very unique Giants' medal on your collar. I have been a fan all my life and have never seen one. May I inquire where it came from?"

"Of course," the Whippet replied. "This is an award I received from the Giants for some past accomplishments. I treasure it because it was given to me by a good friend of mine by the name of Bob Lurie."

Sam swallowed the water in his throat for the second time, even though he didn't have any water in his mouth.

"Bob Lurie?" he thought to himself. "The past owner of the Giants, Bob Lurie? Wow!" He wondered what the whippet's past accomplishments were, but decided to not ask the question, as it felt awkward.

"That is fantastic," Sam replied. "Mr. Lurie is the reason the Giants stayed in San Francisco in the early '90s. None of the current success would seem as exciting if they were the Tampa Bay Giants."

"Well said," the Whippet replied. "My name is John, but most people call me J.W."

"Nice to meet you, J.W. My name is Sam, and I am headed to the game today. I have an extra ticket to The Patch; would you like to join me?"

J.W. thought about it for a second and then smiled. "Sure, I haven't been to one of the playoff games, and it would do me well to get down to the park."

While some of Sam's other encounters with his ballpark companions had been awkward, this union was smooth from the beginning. The two dogs continued their conversation as they started towards the game. They walked down Clay Street amidst the apartments and descended through China Town, passing the Transamerica Pyramid.

Initially, they discussed the pitching match-up of Matt Cain versus Cole Hamels. J.W. seemed to be especially interested in the poise and confidence with which the Giants were performing. Sam was very concerned about the top of the Phillies' line up. Rollins, Victorino, Polanco, Utley, and Werth – all could take a pitch up in the zone and turn it into extra bases, or worse. This had the lab worried, as the Giants had struggled to generate runs and with Hamels on the mound. Getting to four runs seemed impossible.

J.W. was less worried about the Phillies and preferred to focus on the preparation that Bruce Bochy and his coaching staff had been working on all season.

"The hay is in the barn," he said.

The conversation changed a bit as they reached the water at the Ferry building and joined the throng of fans heading to the park. Sam told J.W. about his efforts with the Water Dog Rescue Society and how it had changed his life. J.W. was fascinated to hear what Sam was learning. Sam shared how his love of the water was so natural for him and how well his rescue training was going. J.W. encouraged Sam to seek to understand his teammates' needs and to make sure he paid attention at all times.

"Your ability to be alert and then take quick action is a crucial skill to have," J.W. said as they passed underneath the Bay Bridge.

The line outside Red's Java house was down the street, and they even had to wait a bit to get a drink of water from the bowl Red left for dogs.

The final half mile along the Embarcadero was covered by the largest crowd Sam had ever seen. He was sure that "The Patch" would be packed, and he was excited to introduce J.W. to the boys at the club. Sam hadn't told anyone at The Patch about his interesting viewing locations within the stadium and about his former guests. He didn't want to upstage any of the older members. But he thought J.W. would certainly know a few of his friends, and he was excited about the thought of making the connection.

As they reached the Orlando Cepeda statue at the corner of Second and King Street, J.W. turned to Sam and said, "Sam, let's see if we can find a new spot for you to watch the game from. I have a few friends up in the press box. My guess is that watching a game from there would be fun for both of us."

"Wow, that would be great," Sam replied. "I have never seen a game from there."

Inside, Sam was laughing to himself. Of course J.W. had a fantastic new place for him to watch from! In the past several months, he had been in the centerfield tower and the dugout. Now he was heading to the press box. What was next, the field?

J.W. led Sam to the club gate on the Third Street, and the security guard smiled and waved at J.W. in the same way he would have said hello to Willie Mays. Sam's patch pass was enough for entry to the park, and they were shortly at the entry to the press room.

The next fifteen minutes were unlike any Sam had ever experienced. Inside the press box, J.W. was revered. Sam saw every writer and sportscaster that followed the Giants all address J.W. as "Mr. Wooden" with reverential tones. Sam knew the media professionals to be witty, articulate, and even crass. He had never heard these types of tones and words come out of their mouths. About the third time he heard the words "Mr. Wooden," it dawned on him who his new friend was, and he couldn't believe his fortune.

John Wooden was the greatest coach of the twentieth century, and he had won ten NCAA titles in basketball. The sports writing community was a small one, and, even though his titles were in a different sport, they knew when they were in the presence of greatness.

Just as J.W. had surmised, he and Sam were shown seats. The press room seats were sandwiched between the lower box seats and the club level. They offered the scribes access to the game at just above field level. These were some of the best sightlines at AT&T Park, and, for today's mid-day match up, the East Coast media had descended on San Francisco in full force.

Much of the buzz centered on the future. In the American League, the Yankees were playing the Texas Rangers. The prospect of a New York versus Philadelphia series was all the out of town writers could talk about. Spending three days in S.F. was a nice vacation for the baseball establishment, but they didn't expect to be back for the World Series. The Phillies would take two out of three in S.F. and head home only needing one win to clinch the National League Pennant.

Sam and his new friend and coaching superstar, J.W., settled in as Cain and the Giants took the field on another sunny and brisk San Francisco day. Cain was dealing from the beginning, giving up only two hits over seven innings of shutout baseball. The Giants squeezed out three runs from Cole Hamels, and Javier Lopez and Brian Wilson pitched complete innings to earn the Giants a crucial win, taking a two-one series lead.

The press room was buzzing about the pitching for the Giants. Everyone wondered whether the Giants could catch lighting in a bottle and pitch lights-out. Anything was possible! The reality of the Phillies' bats coming to life was thought to be a fait accompli, but, if they remained silent, this could be the Giants' year!

J.W. and Sam eased out of the press room and fell in with the flow of the crowd. Sam was sure that this was the Giants' year.

"J.W., how did you have so much success as a coach, and what do you think about this year's Giants team?"

A small smile came to J.W.'s face as he received the question. It was a smile that said, "Son, I have lived my whole life in such a way that my actions would be true to my values and that, from time to time, that question might be asked of me."

"Sam, I have a few thoughts on the subject of success, which I will address in a minute. As for the Giants, I like their spirit, and I really like the poise of a pitcher like Matt Cain. I don't know if they will beat the Phillies or win the World Series, but I like what I see. Now back to this word, 'success.' From the sounds of things, you are in the midst of your own title run with your Water Dog Rescue Society efforts, and I think we might have an interesting discussion on the walk home."

Sam, feeling like some great wisdom was about to come his way, was fully alert and paying attention. "That sounds great," Sam said.

J.W. started with a story. "I was coaching at Dayton College many years ago and was working with my students in both the classroom and the gym. I was dedicated to helping them learn, and I would give them grades based upon where they were at the time of the test. I also gave my basketball players grades in the form of playing time. The shock I received was that the parents very much felt my choices were permanent and final. Worse yet, they would turn on the child and affix the 'C' grade as a negative label. This would in no way help my student.

"As a coach, I also noticed that, regardless of circumstance, my success was ninety percent or more correlated to my won-loss percentage. This frustrated me because I was focused on our long-term success and the development of our players. Oftentimes, the other team would be at a different point in their development or have more experience. The loss to me was not of consequence if we learned from it. Once again, the fans could not see this at all and only look at the result of the game they had witnessed. However, unlike the classroom where just the student received a label, in basketball both coach and player were fair game."

Sam interjected, "That doesn't seem right."

Smiling, J.W. continued, "Well, right or wrong, it is a timeless challenge for anyone who chooses to compete. All these years later, I still see it played out on sports fields across America."

"So what did you do to have so much success despite that challenge?" Sam probed.

"Well Sam, I decided to take pieces of advice from some of my own coaches, and I came up with my own definition of success that I would live by regardless of circumstance. Because I was a teacher *and* a coach, I needed to have a way to illustratively share what I felt each of my players could become. It took me some time, but, back before I had won a single championship, I started creating the image of a pyramid of success."

"A pyramid?" Sam asked.

"Yes, like the ones in Egypt. They are amazing architectural feats and make for an easy image to remember. It wasn't perfect from the beginning, and I kept working on it my entire coaching career. But the real key was that I had created my own internal definition and process for success. I was willing to live by it, teach it, and deal with any consequences from the outside definitions of success, such as my won-loss percentage."

Sam was glued to what J.W. was saying. The insight that he had into the challenges of the word 'success' were baffling to him at first, but now he just wanted to know more.

"Tell me more about the pyramid," Sam said.

"As it stands today, the pyramid has five layers. The first two are focused on individual attributes, and the next two address how a group needs to function together and to compete. The final layer – the goal – is competitive greatness."

Not wanting the modest grey whippet to stop there, Sam suggested, "It seems that we are just a few blocks away from the Nob Hill Café. Why don't we stop there? If you wouldn't mind telling me more about the entire pyramid, I would really appreciate it."

J.W.'s facial expression was that of a mature teacher being asked to go over the lesson plan one more time by an eager student. He loved being asked that question and responded in the affirmative.

"Of course, Sam. Sharing this with you is what my life has been about."

J.W. continued as they made their way to the café. "The bottom layer has two cornerstones that are the structural underpinnings for all the remaining layers. In the bottom left is 'Industriousness,' and in the bottom right is 'Enthusiasm.' People who display these traits are easy to spot, as they have a spring in their step and they are constantly busy working on improvement.

"In between Industriousness and Enthusiasm are three team-oriented traits: 'Friendship,' 'Loyalty,' and 'Cooperation.' Combining the two edges with the three internal traits creates a person who has a heart or a spirit for almost any task.

"As a coach, I always started with the heart of my players. Our journey as a team each year was going to have many ups and downs. And if we hadn't addressed these issues both individually and as a team, I found things would unravel when it mattered most at the end of the season."

Sam thought of the Giants and all the years he had watched the team compete. He wasn't so sure that the Bonds' era had all these traits, but, watching this year's team in the context of this pyramid, he could see how Bruce Bochy and some of the culture keepers like Huff and Burrell had the spirit of the club focused on helping each other through any challenge they faced.

The two dogs had now found the same spot they had met at just seven hours earlier. With a nice dinner crowd being served, they relaxed at the corner, and Sam nudged J.W. to continue.

"What about the second layer?" the young dog asked.

"The next layer is a study of the mind," J.W. offered. "It has four traits, and they build from left to right. They are 'Self-Control,' 'Alertness,' 'Initiative,' and 'Intentness.'"

Sam thought about the word 'self-control,' and his mind went to his training with Water Dog Rescue Society rescues. Maintaining his composure was key in an emergency situation, and he wondered if this could be similar to what J.W. was explaining.

The whipped continued, "The mind that is in sync with the heart has the ability to work very efficiently, and the mind that is either quick to distraction or easily moved to emotion loses critical seconds during competition. This is why we spend so much time on the word 'self-control.' It is vital to work on your ability to focus and not to be baited to emotion by others.

"I found, time and time again, that many physically gifted athletes came to me with little to no mental self-control. My challenge was that I knew we would never get anywhere without minds to match our bodies. Thus, much of the early part of the season was spent in this area.

"Right after the mind that is in harmony with the body comes the challenge of alertness. I can tell when someone has his head in the game no matter what the game. Watching you today, Sam, it is clear that you are alert to the Giants and the Water Dog Rescue Society, and that made our chance meeting so easy for me. You were into the game, and you were very open and respectful to an old, small dog such as me. I really appreciated that."

Sam beamed, "Thanks, J.W. I have had quite a year so far, and it makes me smile to hear you say that. Tell me more about Initiative."

Continuing, J.W. said "Self Control and alertness are nothing without the courage to take action. The timid mind will hurt the team more than most people understand, as fear of failure can be very contagious. Thus, we always praised initiative; it is the right type of contagious attitude to have on the team. Of course, right after you take action, you will eventually feel the sting of failure or disappointment, and that is why I have Intentness as the final trait of the second layer. Learning how to persevere is a lifelong pursuit and becomes more important as the season and life progresses.

"Take the 2010 Giants as an example: almost every player or coach on this team has faced massive challenges to get to this point in their careers. Furthermore, the Giants have had to trade Bengie Molina, Jeremy Affeldt has gone on the disabled list, and Dwaine Kuiper has coined the term 'Torture' to go with how the team wins. In addition, inside the clubhouse, the slogan is "Pick Up The Guy Behind You." When you pick someone up, they have fallen, and that is the very definition of learning to persevere."

Sam was right in step with every word; all the baseball he had followed now made much more sense to him. The ability to work through a challenge both individually and corporately had lots to do with the mindset of the players. He thought back to what Big Joe had said about the importance of self-talk. Now, while listening to J.W., he saw how a team that practiced those traits all season would be a very tight group.

"Thus, the second layer ends with the combination of a person and a team that have their hearts and minds set on a task and are committed to facing challenges together. Now as a leader, it was my job to help them practice and prepare for the upcoming season within the context of these two layers. The third layer addresses how we practiced collectively."

Sam was familiar with practice because of his recent efforts in the water, and he understood how important practice was for his mind as well as his body. He was curious what J.W. would share when it came to how a team practiced.

"What was your key to a good practice?" he asked.

"Well for one thing we always started on time."

J.W. remarked quickly with a bit of the old coach coming out of him in his tone. Catching himself, he calmed a bit and continued. "The third layer consists of 'Condition,' 'Skill,' and 'Team Spirit.' The team that has practiced the correct amount and taken care of their bodies off the court will be in good condition. What we practiced and how we focused on certain elements of the game made a big difference in our skill levels as well. Finally, team spirit was a magic element in our process because, when the team is the focus, a multitude of individual problems fall by the wayside. Our teams worked hard, practiced the right things, and took care to celebrate team efforts. In the end, some of my best memories are from our late season practices. That is where it all fell into place."

Sam thought about the Giants and how J.W. had said, "The hay is in the barn." He was thinking about Bruce Bochy and the type of practices the Giants were having between playoff games.

"I bet the Giants are focused on the team right now," he mused.

"From the looks of Burrell and Huff, along with Brian Wilson, I would say Coach Bochy has them right where he wants them," J.W. confirmed.

Turning back to the story of the pyramid, Sam asked, "What was it like in the big games?"

"Well Sam, it was fantastic, and that is what the final two layers of the pyramid of success are about. The second to last layer includes the words 'Poise' and 'Confidence,' and the top layer is 'Competitive Greatness.' Poise and confidence were guide posts on how to compete, and competitive greatness was the goal."

"Poise and confidence appear to be the same," Sam said.

"They are brothers, but not twins" J.W. said. "When you have poise, you are focused and not easily distracted from the target. Having poise when the pressure is on comes from living out the rest of the traits, and it can be very contagious on a team. We were always looking for our team captains to lead by example in this area."

"What about confidence?" Sam asked.

"If poise is a protein, then confidence is a sugar," J.W. responded. "Sugars are icing on the cake and make things taste sweet, and so is the right dash of confidence. Belief in oneself is vital for accomplishment in any activity, especially when it is rooted in hard earned practice. Your efforts in and around San Francisco with the Water Dog Rescue Society are all giving you a foundation to compete with both poise and confidence. Just remember to stay focused on your game plan and compete with vigor. As you practice, so shall you perform under pressure. The byproduct is often a well-earned victory or accomplishment."

Sam sat up and looked the Whippet in the eye. "J.W., thank you so much for the lesson. I would never have guessed so much went into the role of a coach."

J.W. responded, "My pleasure, Sam. Having an eager student makes it much more fun to discuss. I don't know what is in store for the Giants, but, if you practice the traits I have outlined tonight, I am confident that you will sleep well at night both in mind and body."

Sam responded, "I am going to head home, as I want to think some more about what you have shared. I also want to listen to the post game talk shows, as they should be on fire tonight!"

J.W. was ready to return the goodbye when his eyes shot up, as if he was remembering something. "Oh and one more thing, one of my longtime sponsors had these dog tags made. I think you might benefit from what they say. I hope we can continue our discussions in the future. I found you a most welcome student."

With that, the Whippet handed the lab his dog tag. As Sam turned to climb Russian Hill and drop into the Marina, he looked on the back and read:

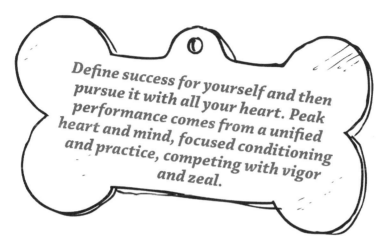

Define success for yourself and then pursue it with all your heart. Peak performance comes from a unified heart and mind, focused conditioning and practice, competing with vigor and zeal.

Feeling as if he was the only person who was having a better season than the Giants, Sam jogged home to place the tag in his doghouse. The front wall was starting to fill up with the tags he had been given by his new friends. He also began to think about the Giants and the possibility that they might make the World Series. Sam didn't want the fall to end, but, if it did, he was sure hoping it would be with a World Series title for his team and his city.

CHAPTER 8
World Series

"They throw the ball, I hit it; they
hit the ball, I catch it."
- WILLIE H. MAYS

November first in San Francisco signals the true end of summer. Many other towns have leaves falling off of trees at this time of year, but, in San Francisco, it begins a six week period where rain can come down in sheets or sun can drench the hills and city sights in almost perfect light.

October of 2010 had been a blur for long-time city residents who were now addressing the very real fact that the Giants were not only in the playoffs, but they seemed to have some momentum. In a game of statistics and long term probabilities, the flukes or breaks made a huge difference to the extremely superstitious players and fans, and the Giants were catching their share of breaks. The result of this was that, for the fan who has no glove or bat in the game but who lives or dies on every pitch, the tension was palpable. Very real as well was the fifty-two year cloud hanging over the franchise. Plenty of stories were being told at coffee shops and bars throughout the city about the disappointments of McCovey's '62 line drive, the "The Humm-Baby" team of '89, and the most recent wound of being seven outs away in '02. For the fan, October of 2010 was delightful, but it had been tense.

Sam, for his part, had his best October ever. The efforts in the bay with the WDRS had culminated with him passing his final tests, and he now wore the same badge on his collar that, back in April, he had noticed Brad the golden retriever wearing. He was now a fully trained rescue dog.

Additionally, the Giants had won the League Championship Series with the Phillies in a tight game six. The Texas Rangers had upset the New York Yankees, and, in the first four games of the World Series, the Giants' bats had come alive. They were now one win away from winning the World Series.

Sam was confident this was the Giants' year; however, he was a nervous wreck inside. Game five was huge because of the "Ghosts of Game Six" in 2002, when then manager Dusty Baker had pulled Russ Ortiz in the seventh, after which the bullpen gave up the lead to the Angels and subsequently lost game seven and the series.

But Sam knew that this team had magic. However, it was also the team whose bats could go so silent and that even one run sometimes felt like an accomplishment. This was the team that, on the fourth of July, had been seven and a half games back in the West and were begging to get in the Wild Card race. This was the team that had lightning in a bottle and, on November first, had their ace Tim Lincecum pitching against Texas ace Cliff Lee in a rematch of game one. This was the team, and this was the moment!

Unfortunately for Sam and the thousands of Giants fans, the game was in Texas, so, in this moment of need and dire importance, all he could do was head down to AT&T Park and commune with the other fans to watch the game on the big screen. The Giants were the best organization in the business, and they loved having people down near their ball park. Sam knew he would need to be next to his fellow fans. The game was set for six pm, so Sam awoke on the first day of November with a plan to patrol the marina during the morning and then head down to the yard in the mid-afternoon.

His morning patrol of the waterfront consisted of the area between Fort Point and Fort Mason. This 2.4 four mile stretch between the two closed military bases was home to several yacht clubs, hundreds of boats, and thousands of citizens exercising along the east to west running shore line. From time to time, Sam would see a boat in trouble out in the bay, and he would alert the coast guard via the alert system set up along his route. Ten years prior, the society had constructed wireless alert boxes that the dogs could use to sound the alarm. Sam would also keep the peace amongst the dogs that were out and about, but his real job was to make sure no one drowned in the water. This mandate included dog or human, and, while Sam had seen a rescue completed in his training, he had yet to be needed in a real disaster.

Ever observant and amped in general, Sam found the job of covering the large expanse a breeze. He had barely a task to complete, and, when he reported back into the control shack at the end of his shift, he remarked to his companions how quiet it had been out there. The responses back surprised him.

"Well, it is all fine now, but, if the Giants win tonight, it could be a different story," was one response.

"We had seven different rescues after the last 49er Super Bowl win," was another retort.

Sam thought, "I had no idea," and with that he wished them luck and began his journey along the Embarcadero.

He passed the entertainment of Fisherman's wharf and Pier Thirty-Nine; he whisked by the Pier Twenty-Three Grill and Red's Java Hut; and he decided to stop for a drink of water at The Delancey Street Café.

CHANGE DOESN'T BITE

The Delancey Street Café was part of a San Francisco non-profit that worked to rehabilitate citizens who had past legal violations. The system that was devised by John Maher in 1971 calls for a series of steps and responsibilities for the recovering people to accomplish as they assimilate into society. One of these steps was to participate in the running of a business. Delancey Street had a series of businesses – a moving company, a Christmas tree operation, and the Delancey Street Café. The Café also had a sit-down restaurant and a book store, but, for Sam's purposes, the Café was the attraction, as it had the water bowl.

The Café sat just three short blocks from AT&T Park, and, even though it was a road game, the streets and stores were filled with fans. By this time, once Sam was at a watering hole, he almost expected to meet someone new. The city of San Francisco had become a very small town for him now, as he had worked almost every district with his Water Dog Rescue Society team. He also felt very confident because of his experiences with Joe and J.W. If in doubt, he opened up to people, and he found they returned the favor.

The café was alive with customers, and, as he walked up, Sam noticed several dogs that he recognized from previous games. All were decked out in Giants' gear, all were fired up for the game, and the mood was festive.

Sam ended up talking quite a bit with a friend from his WDRS work by the name of Jason. Jason was an Australian sheep dog and, while only average in the water, was fantastic at the park patrolling jobs they performed. Jason had come with a pal that was a rather relaxed bloodhound by the name of Reid. Sam was immediately aware that Reid was about the same age as him and, from the looks of it, was a long time Giants fan. They spoke of past events in Giants history with ease, and both felt that tonight's game was critical.

"Ending it with Lincecum on the mound is vital," Reid offered.

Sam agreed, "The last thing we want is to relive a game six. The Rangers' bats are sure to wake up soon."

The hours before game time slipped away quickly. With no game to be played, the Giants had opened up the entire park. Both Sam, his buddy Jason, and Reid agreed that watching the game from the field would be fantastic.

"Just on the edge of the infield at second base will be perfect," Jason suggested.

The three decided to head out right away. Within minutes, they were inside the first archway and could feel the moisture of grass underneath their foot pads. They were joined immediately by thousands of their fellow fans, and, for the fifth time in one season, Sam was going to be watching a game from a different part of AT&T Park.

The minutes leading up to the start of the game from the vantage point of the field were a thrill for Sam. He loved being in the middle of all that energy, and he hoped that, all the way in Arlington Texas at Rangers Stadium, the Giants could feel just a bit of that feeling and bring home a World Series Title.

In Arlington, Bruce Bochy and the Giants were feeling loose and ready to close out the Rangers. The team had hit its stride against the Rangers, and, with Lincecum's control over his new slider, they felt like they had a secret weapon.

The problem was that Cliff Lee was on the mound for the Rangers, and they knew game one had been a fluke.

The first six innings of the game turned out to be exactly what they experts had predicted in game one. Both pitchers were dealing, and the hitters looked foolish. Nary had a runner reached base, and none had yet to be in scoring position.

The top of the seventh inning brought the heart of the Giants line up to face Lee for the third time of the game. Cody Ross led off the inning by hitting a 1-2 pitch up the middle for just the fourth hit of the game. Juan Uribe, who had won a World Series with the White Sox, was up next and on an 0-2 pitch. He singled to center, and, for the first time in the game, the Giants had a runner in scoring position.

The next two batters were Aubrey Huff and Pat Burrell. They had been teammates all the way back in college at the University of Miami. They were also the clubhouse character setters, and they knew this was their time to step up.

Huff did something he had never done in his 6,112 previous at bats; he laid down a sacrifice bunt to move Ross and Uribe both into scoring position, which also set up Burrell to knock them in with just a single or a sacrifice fly ball. Burrell, for his part, had been slumping of late; in fact, his bat had gone ice cold against the playoff caliber pitching. Still, no one brought more determination and grit to the plate than "Pat the Bat."

After a ferocious first pitch swing and a foul ball, he worked the count to 2-1 by letting two Cliff Lee pitches go by. Sadly, in four more pitches, he was walking back to the dugout, bat in hand after striking out on a three-two fastball by Lee.

The Giants' "two on with nobody out" rally was now hanging by a thread with the veteran Edgar Renteria representing their last hope. Renteria had been a solid fielding shortstop for the Giants and was a playoff tested performer, but, despite the home opening heroics, the pop had left his swing, and now all of the Giants' nation was praying for any kind of ball to fall on the outfield grass. Lee missed with two straight pitches, and Renteria stepped out of the batter's box while Lee remained on the rubber. Renteria stepped back in, readied himself, and took the next pitch from Lee. He sent it four hundred four feet over the left centerfield fence for a three-run homerun!

The Giants' dugout went ballistic, homes all over the Bay Area erupted, and it was pure bedlam in AT&T Park. Sam, Jason, and Reid jumped, leaped, and yelped along with fifty thousand other fans as Renteria made his way across home plate. The celebration had to be tempered a bit, due to the fact that it was only the top of the seventh and Aaron

Rowand was in the batter's box to face Lee. Rowand flied to right on the first pitch, and the series was now officially within the Giants' grasp.

Back at AT&T Park, most of the fans were celebrating during the seventh inning stretch and the playing of God Bless America. However, some of the fans, including Jason, Sam, and Reid, knew that nothing was over until the Giants had recorded their twenty-seven out. These would be the hardest nine outs in Giants' history, and the Rangers had homerun power to spare.

Their fears were confirmed when, with one out, Nelson Cruz took a 1-1 offering from Lincecum and sent it three hundred ninety-seven feet into the left field bleachers. The team of Bruce Bochy and pitching coach Dave Righetti had their work cut out for them as they juggled their choices within the Giants' dugout. There was no question who had the ball in the ninth inning, and that it was Brian Wilson's time. However, the five outs that remained became a different story after the very next batter, Ian Kinsler, walked on seven pitches.

Sam and his friends debated it as if they were Bochy and Righetti. Jason wanted to leave Lincecum in. "He looks fine, his pitch count is okay, and he will settle down."

Sam countered, "But you have Javier Lopez for the left-ies and Sergio Romo for the righties. These guys have been unhittable."

Lincecum stopped most of the discussion in either the dugout or between the dogs by striking out both David Murphy and Bengie Molina in five pitches each.

The eighth inning was an inning of little drama and almost less time, as Neftali Feliz retired the Giants in eleven pitches, including an infield single by Buster Posey. Lincecum took the mound with a one-base runner hook from Righetti and responded by taking only nine pitches to retire the Rangers. He floated off the mound into the dugout knowing his night of work was complete.

As if sensing that more runs would mean more time for Brian Wilson to have to wait to pitch, and not wanting to keep the Bearded Bull away from his mound any longer than necessary, the Giants took only twelve pitches to record three outs in the top of the ninth.

The TVs turned to commercials, and everyone in the Giants' fan base all over the world turned to each other and thought of the Dwayne Kuiper coined phrase, "Giants base-ball...Torture!" They hoped and prayed for a one-two-three ninth inning from "B-Weezy."

Facing Wilson in the ninth for the Rangers was the heart of the lineup – Hamilton, Guerrero, and Cruz, who had homered back in the seventh. Wilson made his living off of blistering speed and a cut fastball. However, all three hitters had the skills to take Wilson deep, and everyone watching was excited to see the duels unfold.

Hamilton quickly fell behind 0-2. He fouled off a pitch and then amazingly looked at strike three. His return to the dugout meant the Giants were two outs away. Vladimir Guererro swung one of the heaviest bats in the majors and was a notorious first ball and bad ball hitter. True to form, he barely settled in before swinging at the first pitch, grounding it to Edgar Renteria at shortstop to record the second out.

Now the Giants were one out away, and in stepped Nelson Cruz. He, too, seemed to be ready for a passive at bat when he let the first pitch go by for a strike. The next pitch was a ball, and the count moved to 1-1. The third pitch offered was where the at-bat got serious, when he just missed with a strong swing. The count was 1-2; the Giants were one strike away! All Wilson had to do was get one strike, and it would be over. Fifty-two years of San Francisco Giants torture would be gone, and all the ghosts of past failures would be erased. They were one strike away!

Wilson's next two pitches were offered, and, in a show of good judgment, Cruz let them go by. Both were called balls. Cruz had now worked the count to his favor, and, with just a two run lead, he knew that Wilson would not want to let the tying run reach the plate. Ian Kinsler was due up, and, while he was no Josh Hamilton, Cruz knew the next pitch would have to be a good one.

Strutting around the mound like a bull, Wilson found the rubber, received his sign from Posey, and threw his eleventh pitch of the inning. Cruz appeared to be committed to swing from the very beginning. The ball missed Cruz's bat, or Cruz's bat missed the ball, which found its way into Buster Posey's catcher's glove for a swinging strike three. The rookie catcher leaped in the air and cleared home plate in a second. He was carrying Brian Wilson shortly thereafter, as the Giants players rushed the mound to celebrate their World Series title in the heart of Rangers Stadium.

Sam, Jason, and Reid joined in with the throng of fans for the celebration of their lives. All of them now had a new family, consisting of the total number of fans who had watched the Giants win the series at AT&T Park. The story of the game had so much in common with how the Giants had won games all season, timely if absent hitting combined with stellar pitching. This, coupled with a clubhouse that had a fraternity house atmosphere, emboldened teammates to stay loose and play hard. How else do you explain Renteria telling leadoff hitter Andres Torres before the game that he was going to hit a home run off of Cliff Lee when he had hit only two since April twenty-seventh? The Giants had cracked the code of modern day baseball, and, in a total team effort from owners to general manager to coaches to players, they would have World Series rings to show for it.

As the three dogs filed out of the stadium and worked their way back to the Delancey Street Café, Sam kept hearing Reid say, "They did it! They cracked the code!"

They had found a spot to sit, and things calmed down a bit. When they could actually hear each other, Sam turned to Reid and asked, "What do you mean they cracked the code?"

Reid smiled and said, "They adapted to the changes in their environment and developed a competitive advantage, which included building a team around their home ballpark. The leadership used their networks to acquire the correct talent and to hire the coaches to train the talent. They then put the team through a series of challenges so that the players were ready for the stress that comes from playoff baseball. This Giants team is such a great example for any business or group to learn from."

Jason turned to Sam, who was a bit confused by what Reid was talking about and said, "Reid is a venture capitalist; he sees things through a different lens."

Chuckling, Reid said, "Sorry, Sam. I love this team, and I love helping people build great companies. Watching the Giants come together appears to many to be catching lightning in a bottle, but my bet is that Giants' President Larry Baer and General Manager Brian Sabean have been working on this ever since they didn't renew the Bonds contract in '07. I am so happy for them because it appears they are set up to continue to invest in young solid pitchers. And with this ballpark, that is a really good strategy."

Sam liked the sound of that, and he liked the thought of the Giants getting back to the playoffs in the future. The other parts were confusing to him through. But if he had learned anything from this Giants season, it was to ask strangers to share their thoughts with him, as he always learned something.

"Reid, would you mind sharing a bit more about your thoughts on change? I have had a lot of positive changes going on in my life this year and would like to hear more."

Reid looked at Jason, and Jason assured him that he was eager to listen as well. Then Reid dived in. "I have lots of thoughts in this area, but for tonight I will focus on just a few key points. The first is that your influence is greatly tied to the people you know and who they know. We would have never met today if it wasn't for Jason, and I am privileged to meet a member of the Water Dog Rescue Society. The second is that, while knowing a lot of people is nice, having extremely strong relationships with fewer people can be just as beneficial. Finally, you must have a system in place to measure success as you define it and to adapt to the changes that occur around you."

Continuing, Reid shared, "Let's take the Giants as examples of each point. The General Manager, Brian Sabean, is one of thirty people with his job, and he is, in fact, now the longest tenured GM in the Majors. Many of the people who have worked for him are now working at other teams, and some have even gone on to be General Managers themselves.

"Another key group of baseball professionals are the scouts. For decades, scouts have traveled all over the world on behalf of their club in search of talent. In some cases, these scouts become very tied into the cultures that the young players came from and the relationships that were crucial to landing the player. Sabean's tenure means he also knows more scouts than his competition. In a word, Sabean is networked.

"Thus, when the Giants started to move away from their Barry Bonds focused club, they probably looked at their ballpark and backed into a strategy. Bonds was a once in a generation player, and he packed the house with his batting prowess. However, the team had Bonds when they built the ball park, and it became quite clear that right field was not a home run hitter's delight. The Giants' front office had to know that the post-Bonds era would be pitching focused.

"The Labor contracts in baseball dictate long-term planning that has to start years in advance. This is where Sabean's network comes into play. He only has a finite amount of resources; with those resources, he needs to have chemistry in the clubhouse and keep the peace with the ever watchful fans. When he allocates poorly to a free agent, it can set the team back quite a few years. Therefore, he needs to acquire players from other teams and sign new talent into his farm system with good judgment. The better his network, the better intel he has on what other teams are focusing on, and how they value a player might be different than how the Giants view that same player."

Sam, who had been following along step by step, interjected, "So, since the Reds play in the Great America Ball Park and it is a home run hitter's ball park, they will undervalue a fly ball pitcher like Matt Cain and be more apt to sign a pitcher with a little more sink in his pitches like Bronson Arroyo."

"Precisely," Reid said.

Jason, jumping into the dialogue, said, "Or those same Reds might want to have a stronger hitting line up and therefore spend more of their money on power in the lineup than the pitching staff. Thus, the Reds' GM and Sabean might be able to trade more easily because, while they are both playing baseball, the ballparks dictate different strategies."

"Exactly," Reid answered.

"The eighty-two home games are a significant part of the schedule, and each ballpark has its quirks. AT&T Park is a huge home-field advantage for the Giants, but only once they created a team to fit the ballpark. Sabean has done that year by year, and 2010 was the payoff."

"But how does what you were saying about a quality network make a difference in this case?" Sam asked.

"Without getting too technical on a night for celebration, I have noticed, time and time again, that the quality of your relationships is far more important than the number of relationships. Let's take Sabean's relationship with scouts as an example. He needs to be friendly with almost all scouts, but his best intel is going to come from a few close scouts whom he can really trust. The dollars he has to allocate to unproven prospects are so precious that it is better for him to have a few tight relationships than sprinkling his efforts over a multitude of scouts. Right now, Sabean's top scout is Dick Tidrow."

"Wow," Sam said. "I never looked at it like that before."

Reid turned to him and shared, "Now this doesn't mean you aren't building and growing the number of people you know. It is just that, when you are planning a strategy for any endeavor, it is best to start with a small, committed group of people."

"That group was Peter Magowan, Bill Neukom, Larry Baer, Brian Sabean, Bruce Bochy, Dave Righetti, and a few scouts," Jason said.

"I would agree with that," Reid said, "and I imagine there are a few people behind the scenes that we are not aware of who played key roles."

Sam, feeling like he was getting some great insights into team building and competition, wanted more. "What about your last point, about having a system wide approach to change?"

Reid, by this time, was really geared up and was ready to explain what he felt was the keystone.

"Thanks for keeping me focused, Sam. The system wide approach to change is a game changer for any organization in our modern economy. The rate at which things have been changing in our economy has increased dramatically, and most groups have been slow to adapt. One of the primary reasons groups are slow to adapt is that change is typically viewed as a one-way street headed in a bad direction. Thus, the more things can stay the same, the better, and a culture gets created that fears change of any kind."

Sam thought for a moment about when someone had tried to introduce a new collar rack at "The Patch." The standards committee had quickly acted to establish that the old rack was fine, and the member was heavily encouraged to not bring any new ideas to the club in the future.

Continuing, Reid said, "The key for the Giants is that they adapted to their new ballpark with a new slant towards the type of ballplayer they drafted. They also shifted to a new manager in Bruce Bochy. Baseball may seem as if it's never changing, but the front office is constantly moving players within the established employment rules of the latest collective bargaining agreement. Bochy, Sabean, and a few others are forced to be aware of the short-term goals and the long-term needs of the club. The outside forces are injury and what the divisional rivals are doing with their teams. The schedule dictates that the Giants play the Diamondbacks, Padres, Rockies, and the dreaded Dodgers forty-four percent of the year. This frequency of competition lends itself to paying close attention to what the other clubs in baseball are doing. Outside change happens almost every week and sometimes daily, and I think other industries and organizations could take a page from the Giants."

Jason remarked, "They cracked the code indeed. It all seems so simple the way you outlined it, Reid."

"I wish it were," the bloodhound responded.

"The practice of this philosophy is where the focus needs to be, and the competition is fierce. I am just so happy for the entire Giants fan base and the leadership that the World

Series trophy is headed to San Francisco. They have been working towards this day ever since they broke ground at AT&T Park in 1999."

The three dogs said their goodbyes as the Café was closing down, and Sam went off down the Embarcadero on his way home. His head was swimming with Reid's thoughts. He had not thought about his relationships in the context of a network, and, although he was naturally a pack-oriented animal, he had been away from his family for so long that he wasn't sure if he had a close group.

As he came along the water, he noticed the party boats all along the bay and was struck by how many boats there were. "Those guys on patrol were right," Sam thought. "There are bound to be accidents with this much boat traffic."

His thoughts about his responsibilities with the Water Dog Rescue Society and his musings on his conversation with Reid and Jason started to gel. He realized that the Water Dog Rescue Society helped him address his questions on Reid's first two points. On his individual patrols and his team safety projects, he was always meeting new people. His second thought was that his small network of close relationships was perfect for his fellow rescue dog network. Smiling with the knowledge that he could put his new strategies to work, he thought about a way to consistently check his progress.

This stumped him a bit, but eventually he pieced together a plan. If he combined everything he had learned from his mentors, he might just have his own system. "I will take one thing from each of them," Sam thought, "and that will allow me to stay on my path while still being flexible to outside forces."

He thought about Brad, and immediately the thought of "Notice More" came to mind. Rephrased as a question, he would ask himself, "am I listening in a curious manner and using all my surroundings in my engagements with others?" Sam thought that, if he asked himself that question twice a year, it would be a good reminder to stay observant.

His thoughts then turned to Big Joe, and he recalled the challenge to be "Others Focused" and being empathetic by having a cause greater than himself. Posed as a question it could be, "am I looking at things from others' point of view when I interact with them" and "am I advancing a cause I care about?"

Sam felt that he was off to a good start as his thoughts turned to D.P. and Sir Ken and that great game he had watched from the Giants' dugout. Sir Ken was always curious about where a dog was intelligent and how individuals and groups work together for a common purpose. Sam thought a good question might be, "what do you have a knack for, and how are you practicing and improving that in which you have natural ability?"

J.W. was still so fresh in his mind that it was easy to remember his building blocks of success. He decided a good question would be, "how are you combining your heart and mind to focus your efforts on individual and team goals so that you may compete to your fullest?"

By adding these four questions together with Reid's focus on being aware of outside forces that need to be listened to, he felt as if he had the makings of a good system that he could hone in the coming years.

Sam noticed a spring in his step as his mind had resolved an internal quandary or puzzle. And he had done all of this from the Delancey Street Café to Red's Java House!

He had just crossed under the Bay Bridge when his ears were alerted to a sudden yelp coming from the direction of the bay. Sam's internal instincts kicked into action, and he immediately triangulated with all his senses and caught sight of a small dog falling off a party boat a few hundred yards from the Embarcadero. Sam looked to see if anyone on the boat had noticed, but, to his further alarm, the boat was moving away from the dog as it was returning its guests somewhere to the north.

With no one else to help and the nearest emergency pole too far away, Sam looked behind and picked the top of the Rincon Tower and then looked forward towards Yerba Buena Island for another landmark that was in line with where he had seen the dog go in the water. With his sightlines established, Sam leapt into the water as only a Labrador retriever can and started swimming towards his target on the far off island.

Sam knew that most dogs can swim, but some of the small breeds would have great difficulty in the cold and choppy waters of the bay. Within five minutes, Sam was upon the other dog. As he got closer, he could see the animal was very small and in quite a bit of duress. Sam immediately began following his protocol and was barking orders to the victim to remain calm and that he was trained to rescue him. To his complete shock, when he got close enough to the dog, he saw that it was none other than his old flat mate Larry!

Larry was in a real panic. He didn't know how to swim, and the boat traffic and the chop from the waves had him very disoriented. He was struggling to keep his nose above water when Sam came upon him and continued his rescue protocol. Sam repeated his directions three times.

"Larry! You are going to be okay. I am a certified Water Dog Rescue Society member, and I am going to bring you to safety."

Larry was in such a panic that he didn't initially pick up what Sam said, or that Sam was the one saying it. However, by the third time, it sunk in, and he said, "Sam? Sam what are you doing out here? Now we are both in trouble!"

Without flinching or responding to Larry, Sam swam into Larry from the left side. With a precision that comes from practice, he grabbed the thick part of Larry's neck and his collar. His grip was firm enough to immediately move Larry in the correct direction, keep his head above the water, and allow him to breathe. Sam was pointed in the direction of safety as he made his move and, with Larry securely in his grasp, started swimming back to land.

Not much transpired in the seven minutes that Sam navigated the bay waters with a mouth full of Larry's neck and collar. Larry's panicked state started to ease as they reached the steps that allowed them to both climb back onto the Embarcadero. Both dogs were spent in different ways as they wiggled and shook the cold bay waters from their coats. Sam had adrenaline running through every vein from the exercise and the emergency rescue he had just successfully completed. Larry's adrenaline came from the panic of falling off a boat. He was weathered from the bay, and his despair from being in the cold water and the ensuing panic that had set in had caused him to start swimming in the wrong direction. The two dogs stood staring at each other for a few minutes. As the moment passed and they both realized they were safely back on land, they smiled and embraced.

Larry spoke first. "Sam, how on earth did you learn to do that? Thank you so much! You saved my life!"

Sam, still shaking his coat from head to toe, responded, "Larry, it is so good to see you. I have thought of you all year. My owners bought me a new dog house that had a radio, so I could follow the Giants. And your pass to The Patch ended up introducing me to a couple of mentors. One of these mentors suggested I join the Water Dog Rescue Society. I took to it easily and have had a great time working with my new team as we patrol the city."

With a sheepish grin, Larry smiled. "You know, Sam, I am sure glad you took the chance to join, or I would have drowned out there tonight. You are a true Labrador retriever, and I am glad you are using your natural skills. This past year, I have thought of you often as I have been adjusting to the ranch I live on in Fresno. We have all kinds of dogs that do a wide variety of jobs. I have come to learn how we are all made for different purposes. While we were living together, I wanted to have you conform to my style of life so it would be easier for me. That was selfish of me, and for that I would like to apologize."

Sam responded, "Thanks, Larry. I have had an amazing year and learned and seen so many new things. I would love to share some of it with you. Why don't we walk back to our flat and get you back to your owners. I am sure my owners will know how to get a hold of them."

"Sounds great," Larry responded, "but we also have to talk about the Giants – what a year! But I am worried about how Sabean is going to keep that pitching staff intact. I am not sure they have the money to do it."

The two dogs took off down the Embarcadero, one a ninety pound chocolate lab with muscles everywhere and a chest almost two feet wide, the other a twelve pound pug that had a hitch in his step and was no more than eighteen inches tall. They were an odd looking pair, they always had been, but anyone could see they were friends.

YOUR PERSONAL SYSTEM
FOR ADAPTING TO CHANGE

Step 1

Incorporate the Principals of Improv

Key Phrase:
> Notice More

Key Question to stay on track:
> Am I listening in a curious manner and using all my surroundings in my engagements with others?

Step 2

Work on getting your head and heart aligned

Key Phrase:
> Be Others Focused

Key Question to stay on track:
> Am I looking at things from others point of view when I interact with them, and am I advancing a cause I care about?

Step 3

When working with others look for their talents

Key Phrase:
> Where are you intelligent?

Key Question to stay on track:
> What do you have a knack for, and how are you building upon that skill with diligent practice?

Step 4
Build your personal plan for excellence

Key Phrase:
Create a personal definition of success

Key Question to stay on track:
How are you combining your heart and mind to focus your efforts on individual and team goals so that you may compete to your fullest?

Step 5
The power of a personal network

Key Phrase:
Build a small team of trusted allies and have a system in place for recognizing and adapting to change.

Key Question to stay on track:
Have the rules of the game I am playing changed and what are my allies noticing?

CHAPTER MENTORS

CHAPTER 4
Brad Robertson
On Your Feet
www.oyf.com

CHAPTER 5
Joe Ehrmann
Coach For America
www.coachforamerica.com

CHAPTER 6
Ken Robinson
www.sirkenrobinson.com

Daniel Pink
www.danpink.com

CHAPTER 7
John Wooden
www.coachwooden.com

CHAPTER 8
Reid Hoffman
The Start Up of You
www.startupofyou.com

ABOUT THE AUTHOR
Drew Sanders

Drew Sanders is a husband and father of two children. He has been adapting and learning his way to successfully running an insurance brokerage practice and has completed several team open water swims across Lake Tahoe and the Maui Channel.

Drew is the founder of the California Season of Life Foundation, a senior member of The Guardsmen of San Francisco, and a board member for his local First Tee chapter. All of these efforts focus on helping disadvantaged youth redirect their futures through positive role models and values based curriculum.

A lifelong lover of reading, Drew found himself learning from a series of authors and the idea of combining their lessons into a story came to mind. Emboldened by the urge to lead by example for his children and encouraged greatly by his wife, mother, and father he has penned his first story for your enjoyment. For Drew, life changes every day, and he welcomes your contribution and perspective on the subject at www.changedoesntbite.com.

2618052R00071

Made in the USA
San Bernardino, CA
14 May 2013